All rights in the printed messages are held by the author Paulette Marie Reymond. This work must only be reproduced with the author's permission, even in excerpts.

Copyright © 2020 Paulette Marie Reymond

Website: https://www.paulette-marie-reymond.com
Email: contact@paulette-marie-reymond.com

Original title:
Vereinigung der Populationen der Inneren und der Äußeren Erde –
Rodon von Agartha spricht zu den Menschen der Äußeren Erde

Translation: Translingua AG
https://www.translingua.ch

Cover design: Katja Jost
https://www.katjajost.ch

Print and distribution: Amazon KDP

ISBN paperback: 9798603233635

Also available as a Kindle eBook.

Reunification of the Populations of Inner and Outer Earth

***

Rodon of Agartha Speaks to the Humans of Outer Earth

channelled by Paulette Marie Reymond

About the Author

Paulette Marie Reymond lives in Switzerland. She has two adult daughters. For 30 years, she has been working as a Channel with the spiritual hierarchy of Earth, the Archangels, high cosmic entities and cosmic siblings.

She wants to support Earth and her people in this time of ascension to a new octave of being.

Website: https://www.paulette-marie-reymond.com

For my beloved grandchildren.

Table of Contents

Preface	1
Rodon of Agartha introduces himself	5
Introduction	7
Compromises	10
Bright Insights	14
The Establishment of Light on Earth	21
Dissolving Negative Influences	28
Red Crossings	35
Necessities	41
From the Inside to the Outside	45
Excesses Inside and Outside	50
Earth – Gaia – Terra	57
Feasibility	64
The Path of Light	76
Tangibility	82
Of the Endless Expanse of the Human Consciousness	88
The Implementation of Your Wishes	94
Purposeful Actions	99
Eyes of a Seer	106
Agartha, a Supreme Land	112
Diverse Intentions	122
Effects on Earth and Her Inhabitants	129
Alterations	137
No Compromises	145
Supplies	153

Effects of Interstellar Communication	**161**
The Last Piece of the Puzzle	**167**
Criteria for the Future	**177**
Diverging Energies	**183**
Acceptance of the Inevitable	**191**
Five-Dimensional Vibration Levels	**198**
The Interplay of Worlds	**208**
Acknowledgement	**217**
Other Books by the Same Author	**218**

Preface

Mother Earth called to me while I was hiking in the Swiss Alps in September 2009. My inner voice urged me to telepathically connect to her, so I went to find a suitable spot. I soon discovered just the right place along a path through a large field in a well-known holiday spa town. My companion gave me the protection I needed, and I connected with Gaia. As always, my contact with Gaia was incredibly loving. She immediately sent me on to an entity called Rodon, who desired to speak with me. This was how I first encountered Rodon of Agartha. He told me that the place I had luckily found concealed a gate to Agartha. He asked me if I wanted to work to further the matters of its population. I agreed, and we parted. Despite assuming I wouldn't hear from him for some time, my next contact with Rodon happened back at home, in November of the same year.

In the night from 31 May to 1 June 2010, I felt the presence of St. Germain very strongly. My beloved Master St. Germain has taught and guided me over the past years. He is responsible for my work as a channel. He was already awaiting me when I connected to him. He suggested a nightly walk through a forest-like area, saying that there was something he needed to show me. We walked side by side in silence, until he suddenly pushed aside the branches of a bush and told me to look. There, in the dark, I saw a rock with a moss-covered door. My claustrophobic mind thought: *Oh boy! I hope I won't have to go in there!* To my surprise, the door opened, and a beautiful light shone from it. It was reminiscent of a sunny summer's day. A beautiful man with brown skin (similar to the Maori or the indigenous people of Hawaii) emerged from it. He was young, strong and fit, neither fat nor thin. He was virtually naked. A green scarf was slung around his neck, dangling onto his chest. Another green scarf was wrapped around his waist, dangling between his legs. His face radiated an incredible happiness. His eyes were sparkling, and he had a likeable, broad smile, flashing brilliantly white teeth. In his black hair, he wore some kind of red and green feathers or flowers, like a wreath. His face was so attractive that I did not pay attention to those details.

Stepping out of the door, he approached and embraced me, saying: "It's so good to see you, dear sister." St. Germain and I looked quite pale and boring next to the new man. He was taller than we were, too, standing at about 2 m. I melted in his strong arms! Then I asked him his name, and he replied that it was Rodon and that he was of Agartha. When I asked him about his position in Agartha, he said he was a chief, but we would call him a president. He then asked me if I desired to be part of the merging of Inner and Outer Earth, to which I readily agreed. He let me know that he would contact me towards the end of autumn, in order to write a book about Agartha with me. He wanted to use that book to describe the population of Agartha, and to introduce them to the humans of Outer Earth. Finally, he told me that his body was having trouble with the energy density of Outer Earth, so he sadly had to take his leave. He laid his right palm onto the left side of his chest and said the word "Alao" in farewell. The door closed, and St. Germain and I were standing in the dark again.

I am now aware that I have been prepared for this work for quite some time. In the summer of 2007, I was surprisingly contacted by Quetzalcoatl (Feathered Serpent), who asked me to be in Tikal (Guatemala) on 18 January 2008. We reached the temple area and found a shaman waiting for us, who had been told of our arrival in a dream. He had brought all the ingredients for a fire ceremony. Many toucans gathered in a nearby tree to assist as my dear companion Esther and I experienced a fire ceremony in the temple complex of the Mundo Perdido (the Lost World) on that day *de la fertilización de la tierra* (of the Fertilisation of Earth).

Afterwards, we travelled on to Mexico. We were guided to the destinations of Teotihuacán (Full Moon), Monte Albán, Palenque, Uxmal, Kabáh, Dzibilchaltún, Chichén Itzá (New Moon with Solar Eclipse) and Tulum. We were initiated into Earth with all its populations.

I find my fulfilment in the certain knowledge that I am part of a greater whole. We are all guided and can choose to open the doors that present themselves to us. We can participate in the world's divine orchestration. The main prerequisite to achieve this is a loving heart and trust in All-That-Is.

Dear Reader, I hope that the love of our co-residents of Earth, the population of Agartha, will warm your hearts and that you will be able to perceive Earth as a greater whole through these lines.

We are all ONE
Paulette Marie Reymond

Rodon of Agartha introduces himself

Allow me to introduce myself before you let the contents of this book carry you away. My name is Rodon, and I belong to the population of Agartha, which shares Earth with you. However, we do not live on Outer Earth, but in Inner Earth. This fact alone may be difficult to accept and to comprehend for you. Therefore, we in Agartha have decided to contact our earth siblings in this manner. Your ascension into the Fifth Dimension will soon allow us to reunite to master the terrestrial and cosmic fates of Earth together.

In this book, I represent my people. I am their spokesman and I act in their spirit. All that I say, my brothers and sisters say as well. I maintain a close connection with them at all times. Our society has deeply integrated the 5th dimension, and we are all mentally connected to each other. Therefore, do not see me as a single person, but as all the people of Agartha.

This being said, I greatly hope that you can feel our love for you in this text, and that you will support the reunification of all populations of Terra.

Alao* (*Meaning: wholeheartedly, with all my heart)
Rodon

Introduction

The population of Agartha has been living inside Earth for eons. You may find this surprising to hear. After all, doesn't it go against everything you believed you knew about your Earth, your home planet? Even your sophisticated science has not dealt a lot with your planet so far. The physical laws of Earth and her place in cosmic interaction were its preferred areas of research. Nevertheless, there is a population named Agartha living inside Earth. It is part of the planet. It is part of your home.

The accelerated energy of the last decades has flushed the populations of Outer Earth into the Fifth Dimension, to accompany our planet as it continues its journey into the Light. This evolutionary progress now requires all populations of Earth to unite, no matter if they are living on Outer Earth, or in Inner Earth. All of us are intertwined and will proceed together on our journey into the Light. We are all one, citizens of Earth, of Terra or of Gaia.

How is it possible for a population to live inside Earth? Are they living in the dark? What do they eat? These and many other questions will arise when you think about a population that lives inside Earth.

From your point of view, these questions are justified. After all, you know that Earth is a sphere that the sun shines upon. Do not forget that, not too long ago, you believed Earth to be flat! I will now show you that Earth is more than just a ball hurtling through space.

Earth, with its solar system, travels on a route through the cosmos. She is not bound stationarily to a cosmic region but is drifting ever closer to the Light with its solar family, shifting from one energy density to the next-lighter one. This cosmic journey greatly influences Earth and her populations, subjecting them to continuing evolutionary steps of cosmic proportion. These steps are difficult for your historical records to track. The current lifetime of an individual, or even a human society, is too short to grasp the greater perspectives of the populations. Let me use the lifespan of insects as compared to the life expectancy of a human as a metaphor. An insect will never be able to develop a greater perspective. It will be happy with its time on Earth and adjust its societies to that. Please forgive me for this comparison, but it is the only way that I can take you along onto our journey of

Earth, tell you about my population, the Agartha, and reveal the mysteries of Earth to you.

They truly are mysteries. Now, they will be revealed to Outer Earth. They must be, since we, that is all of Earth, with all her populations, are departing on our further starlit journey into the Light to enable us to merge with the cosmic societies as a reunified single earthly population.

The evolutionary quantum leap mankind of Outer Earth is about to achieve enables this step of revelation. We, the population of Agartha, and I, Rodon, as its representative, look forward to our future meetings and cooperation. We are all united in the Light of the ONE. We are the love of the ONE and will continue our cosmic flight together with all of Earth. We will join the cosmic family as a unified earthly population.

Compromises

Making compromises can facilitate development processes. That does not mean avoiding a process of life, but only admitting part of it in order to move into the required direction step by step. Of course, the entire process of life is a development that must happen over time. The focus one needs, for example, to let go, can only be developed gradually, however.

Sometimes, it can be smarter to make compromises in order to avoid potentially fatal situations.

My people made such a compromise. The living situation on our continents of Mu and Lemuria was threatening our lives and forced us to leave our beloved home behind. A variety of natural disasters, such as torrential rains and seismic activity, drowned our continents in the ocean forever.

Our people were highly spiritual and living on a different energy density than what you are used to on Outer Earth. To my people, the matter of Earth was a living collection of pulsations of Light. It was a matter to be shaped, available to be used by the Light processes of mankind. It merged with them in order to create a new territory. Some of my people did not choose to flee. They wanted to become more closely connected to their home: to Earth. They had no wish to leave the vibrations they had developed together. They wanted to build new opportunities together with Earth. With their joint Light process, they created a new home for themselves in the inner realms of Earth, rather than on her outside. As mentioned already, they had the skill to handle matter and to create and design their home to match their wishes and needs. A considerable share of my people chose this path in order to preserve their spiritual achievements and to flee from the cycle of rising density of matter on Outer Earth.

I started this chapter by mentioning a compromise. Yes, my people chose this compromise. During the entire cycle of extremely high density of matter on Outer Earth, they tried to preserve the amplitude of Earth's vibration, helping to now make a great energetic quantum leap possible for the humans of Outer Earth.

We belong together as one population of Earth. The different vibrational density between our two living areas made it impossible for us to reunite before now. The increase of vibrations that is now happening on Outer

Earth will soon make our vibrational amplitudes compatible, and allow us to embrace each other with open arms.

At the moment, the vibrational density of Outer Earth is still too strong. We must wait for the time that mankind will transform from a carbon- to a crystalline-based form, so that we can continue our earthly presence as equal partners. As I mentioned, this is no longer a matter of centuries. A decade, at most, will be all it takes.

I am telling you all of this in order to prepare you for it. I want to try and expand your borders. I would like to tell you of the connection we have had across eons: the love of our divine creator or God, the great AHAU, is present inside each of us, no matter if we hail from the outer or inner realms of Earth. Our divine creator, God or Goddess, may be called by different names, depending on the culture from which one approaches him or her. We know that we are part of the ONE and accept this as a great responsibility. Our spiritual growth and conscience benefits all of Earth, including the humans of Outer Earth. Divine love is our connection and our future. The more you grow into the Fifth Dimension, the more this statement will become a matter of course.

Let us look into the future confidently and full of love, as we await a new era of Earth.

Bright Insights

This current era is characterised by a great transformation of Earth, be it by fire, flooding, mudslides, seismic activity, or volcanic eruptions. Earth is in motion around the globe. Fire, water and earthquakes change and transform entire regions of Outer Earth. Their severity and cadence are bound to increase as Earth transforms herself anew in order to develop a five-dimensional vibrational density. This great evolution concerns mostly Outer Earth. She must still clear herself of plenty of negative slag from her past. Integrating something new always means letting go of something old in return. You are familiar with this principle from your own living processes. Old, outdated structures must be demolished to form the substrate for building new, contemporary paradigms.

This current era is characterised by intense changes, both in your personal and social areas, and in the Terrestrial one.

We of Agartha are keenly aware of your changes. Terra's changes are ours as well, though not at the same scope as on Outer Earth. We are always in close contact with you, and with former incarnated Agarthans spread all over Outer Earth. Even though their awareness has not yet woken, they are still subconsciously connected to us. Our spiritual development enables us to telepathically attune ourselves to Outer Earth. It will not come as a surprise to you that we also have technical skills. Our evolutionary development has taken us down that path, too. The more Light shares an individual can integrate, the higher their vibrations, the better they are connected to their multidimensional heritage and able to use it. Mankind is making great progress in that area at the moment. Soon, they will take paths that break old borders, renewing their societies along the way.

We have been aware of our brothers and sisters on Outer Earth ever since our retreat into Inner Earth. We have perceived your high cultures and your times of barbarism. Through all of these, however, we have maintained contact with you through our representatives or the spiritual hierarchy of Earth. We always considered us and you to be one single Earthly family, despite our separation in space and dimension. This is why we are overjoyed to soon make this family unification come true. Our love for you is incredibly strong. Our yearning was impossible to quench through all of these millennia.

The pain of our separation will only fade once we are reunified into a single population of Earth. Think of this as you read our words. It is truly a meeting of a currently divided family of mankind. You have experienced this in some countries on Outer Earth. You may be able to understand our pain with that in mind. However, we have never been this close to reunification before. This is why we must make all the necessary preparations now. We will carefully make our first contacts with you, filled with great love and compassion, and handle this reunification process with the utmost care.

Your ancient cultures and today's indigenous peoples have always been, and still are, aware of our presence. Knowledge of us is kept as a great mystery by your secret societies. Believe me that the time of revelation has come, to fully bring the populations of the planet Earth to light. The accelerated energy you are currently exposed to will instil in you a trust and courage in your own history along with an increasing development of consciousness. You will also feel the need to cooperate with us and to see the "other side of the coin". We gladly share our spiritual legacy with you. We can offer tremendous support to Outer Earth in this evolutionary step. Do not hesitate to contact us telepathically. Spin the threads of our shared family network together. Earth, our shared home, will be energetically improved by this, able to broadcast her brilliance into space. Our cosmic siblings will participate in our reunification. This way, they can embrace mankind on Earth as a whole.

Our multidimensional access has allowed us to be in contact with extra-terrestrial societies of Light for a long time. Only as a unified population of Earth will we be able to consciously participate in our cosmic fate and contribute to the committees of Light as a single, unified, mankind.

My dear brothers and sisters of Outer Earth, rouse from your long enchanted sleep to view and enjoy the wonder of our paradise Earth, our shared home, our "spaceship" that leads us further and further into the Light.

You will be granted bright insights into our territory from time to time in future, but only if you integrate into your bodies the high Light particles that are sent to Earth. Your current physical condition does not yet allow you to visit us. The vibrational difference is too great, and your physical constitution would suffer greatly in the process. However, your transition into the fifth dimension and integration of the high cosmic vibrations will enable you to enter our territory in the foreseeable future. We will protect you and take precautions to only allow such visitors who can stand our high vibrations.

This is not some elitist selection, but a proof of our love for our brothers and sisters of Outer Earth. Our energy density should let you soar, rather than make your bodies suffer. As integration of the five-dimensional energy density on Outer Earth progresses, access to our territory will become a pleasure for all visitors. We look forward with great joy in our hearts to that time in which our societies will merge. The time is close now – very close.

Great shared experience will characterise and enrich our future. Trust in this evolutionary process, for it is a great step on our path of Light for both parties. Light and love are our shared foundations on which we found our evolution. Only Light-filled evolution can eventually bring peace and prosperity to people. Peace will spread across all of Outer Earth, allowing her people to develop in safety and prosperity. Spiritual growth will follow all on its own. Fear and an empty stomach are bad advisors on the path of Light.

Now I would like to speak to the more rationally inclined. A time will come when you must put aside the data you have accumulated in your studies in order to acquire new, multidimensional information. You will learn to master your everyday lives with all your senses. You will rediscover matter. The density of matter will change the more Light impulses reach Earth. You will have to learn a new approach to this. Spiritual or Light-filled matter is subject to different paradigms than you are used to. This new access to matter will be baffling and fascinating for you. Handling it will be much easier and allow you to implement designs that seem fantastic or even outright utopian when viewed today. Stay optimistic and face your near future joyfully.

Close integration of the Light process will make it easier for people in a society to live together, to handle matter and to be in contact with our Mother Earth. Our beloved home planet will recover from her strains and be healed, to then support and nurture her populations in turn. We are all living in symbiosis with Mother Earth, only able to develop along with her. We support and help each other. We go on our journey along with her and thank her for everything. The act of loving Mother Earth is holy for the Agarthans. After all, doesn't she represent their right to exist across many incarnations? Agarthans incarnated on Outer Earth are also connected to their home, their planet, by this holy love. You can find many of them in your organisations that strive to protect and heal Earth. Agarthans naturally have a special way of approaching her. Their DNA conceals the entire potential of their people. The Agarthans of Outer Earth will also be made aware of their internal potential. They will awaken when the time has come, so that they can fulfil their tasks. Everyone should be invested in taking care of

Earth. We have no place to go if she refuses us her service! Mother Earth has been incredibly patient with mankind. The future will teach us to develop better protection and care for our shared home, and to celebrate our love for our planet.

Contact Mother Earth, no matter which place you call home. Listen to her words and her language. Let her embrace you and allow you to rest on her motherly bosom. This Earthen energy will stabilise you to let you weather the current chaotic era, and set you on the right path to enlightenment. The Paradise Earth must be conquered by everyone to let them enjoy her riches.

Rejoice in walking your future paths in conscious symbiosis with Earth and enjoying her treasures. Sing her praise as her waters, tress and winds teach you, and let her beauty intoxicate you. Let your hearts come together in her extraordinary heart and feel the tranquillity she gifts to you. This loving relationship will surpass all that you have ever known and make you truly human. My love for Earth is so great and deep that I find it hard to restrain my enthusiasm. I hope that you can feel Rodon of Agartha just the way he is. I thank you with all my heart.

The Establishment of Light on Earth

As I mentioned, we used to be on a progressed Light process back when we were still living on Outer Earth and had already reached the Fifth Dimension. Our astronomers and astrologists knew that Earth, with her solar system, would slowly move away from the Light; and that mankind would drop more deeply into matter, i.e. into a lower vibrational density. For our continued survival, our decision to maintain our five-dimensional vibrational density required us to leave the surface of Earth.

This separation from the rest of mankind caused other highly developed cultures to follow suit. The more "recent" history of Earth offers the examples of the Teotihuacans, the Incans, and the Mayans. Those populations didn't just disappear, but joined us, thanks to their multi-dimensional knowledge of matter. Due to their high vibrations, they were no longer able to survive on Outer Earth. Those people have always been connected to us. Not all of those people took this path. Some of them stayed behind. Free will is the highest law on Earth. Those who remained protected their holy sites, that you can still admire today, where you can feel their high spiritual energy. Lingering in that energy will activate your own multi-dimensional DNA. That energy will meet every visitor at their personal vibrational density, and activate their further Light process. Other holy sites on Earth offer the same potential.

For millennia, vibrations slid into progressively lower amplitudes. As the polarity shears gaped dangerously open, life on Earth became more and more difficult. Your history is, as a result, a collection of violence, lack of respect, and greed.

As our solar system travels from darkness into Light, Earth is once again nurtured with an abundance of bright radiation from space. This Light process is drastically changing your private, social and terrestrial lives, leading you into the Fifth Dimension. Let us call it the five-dimensional gateway, since the Light impulses will continue to shower Earth at this strong amplitude for a while, in order to ensure their integration. You are standing at the beginning of a new dimensional level that will develop continuously over centuries. The common three- and four-dimensional polarity gap will be harmonised. It will bring you the peace and prosperity that you desire.

Some people will find integration of these Light impulses into their bodies and their minds unbearable, and they will prefer to leave this planet. Certain species among the flora and fauna will also not survive the change.

Dimensional changes are, by necessity, incredibly pervasive processes in the matter and mind. They must be taken step by step and with all the requisite calm and serenity. The core of the transition time will span approx. 50 years.

The Light impulses Earth has received from the cosmos over time contain the entire spectrum of Light, with all of its qualities and characteristics. Light splits into various colours when it hits Earth. That Light spectrum will increase even more, and now also send five-dimensional qualities to support you. These are new properties that you need to integrate. Matter is continually spiritualised. This will better enable you to implement your part in creation. Believe me that use of this changed matter will fascinate you and allow you to more easily make your wishes come true. Your bodies are also made of Earthen matter, of course. You will tackle pain and illness by recognising the mental processes underlying them, and find yourself able to heal your ailments. Your bodies will become your true temples of manifestation here on Earth. The evolution of the Light processes will pervade the atomic structure and sustainably change you and your environment.

The current accelerated evolutionary process of mankind of Outer Earth will soon bring us together, and enable us to share our treasures and to create new ones. In contrast to us, you will have the entire experience of the great polarity of the Third Dimension stored in your DNA, along with the unwavering will to return Earth to the Light. Even if you are not yet anchored in the Fifth Dimension, you are specialists in changing dimensions. We respect and love you with our whole hearts for this. We thank you for following this path. We, in turn, will be able to support and help you with any difficulties adjusting to the new, higher energy. Every new level of being must be explored and the tools for it must be developed anew. Move into this new era with all your senses. Open yourselves to the "unimaginable". We will be there, first telepathically, and later physically, to support you to the best of our abilities. Until then, you will have learned to telepathically communicate with us from the level of your hearts. That is the cosmic way of interacting with the societies of Light. We will practice it here on Earth as well. It is a loving relationship with All-That-Is. Misinterpretations from translations are prevented as well. Over time, we will, of course, learn each other's languages and communicate in that manner.

The level of the heart will be your way to communicate. It is the quality of the Fifth-Dimension, its basis, the foundation of its existence, and its future focus.

Love is the very essence of creation. It is the building block on which all else rests and is put into practice. Unconditional love will influence your works and your projects to an increasing extent. It will characterise your interactions. Mutual respect will be the future basis for all levels of society and among all the ethnicities of Earth. Mankind will implement its projects with Earth. Only the support of our dear home planet will make investments sustainable for the benefit of everyone involved. Exploiting your resources and suppressing certain populations will be unthinkable in the new era of Earth. This revolution in your conduct will be brought about by the changing cosmic Light impulses that are now showering Earth. Everyone is exposed to that energy. Everyone will find that the shares of love (Light) in their minds and bodies will rise. This individual Light process will change your societies down to their very foundations. It will enable you to create new and universal structures targeted at your living together as a global mankind and your participation as cosmic citizens.

As you can see, the Light particles are now changing the manner of your being. Some will find this a slower process than others. The discrepancy will be hard on you for a while. Everyone will only integrate as much Light as is good for them. Bodies and minds must be able to keep up with this integration. Continuous and calm integration will move you more quickly towards your goal. Enjoy this time with all your senses and experience your personal change along with that of your surroundings. These are small steps that will have great effects over time. This is not about a race or an attempt to escape into a higher dimension. This is a pervasive, personal Light process that holds an evolution jump in store for you.

As I mentioned, this Light process reaches deeply into every single atom. It activates your DNA and builds your Light body. That Light body will serve you well in future, both on Earth and in the cosmos. The Light body is your own "vehicle". It is your resonance body that is connected to All-That-Is. It is your divine identity.

The Light body is more than just your energy field or your aura. It is your own, very personal, vehicle that will enable you to move between places on Earth – or even through space. It is a collection of the purest energy particles – Light impulses – and represents your energy vibration. Similar to a fingerprint, your Light body is your personal identification. It is something like your Light passport. You will create your own Light body. It is part of the Light processes that you develop by integration of the Light impulses of space.

After millennia of darkness, a new, Light-filled day is dawning for mankind. You must get used to this Light first. You must pay it your full attention to enable you to emerge as a new, changed being and to activate your co-creatorship.

It's a quantum leap from darkness to Light. It's a re-birth into a new level of being, and the goal of your current incarnation. Your efforts have paid off. Your personal harvest has been brought in and the table is richly laid. Enjoy it, with all your senses.

Dissolving Negative Influences

Since the harmonisation process of polarities is progressing, you will soon be freed from the severe negative influences. By negative influences, I mean the destructive, violent, disrespectful, and greedy scenarios that you have been exposed to in the past. The new polarity is, of course, still polar, but it will take on a harmonised form. This means that excess can no longer happen. That incredible change will stabilise your societies and give you the security you need to focus on your further path into the Light. Your path into the Light includes your own Light process and the well-being of your environment, your society, and all of mankind. The Light-full evolution always begins with the individual. From there, it will radiate and change the structures of your societies. Every person is involved in this Light process and will be responsible for their own evolution. Self-responsibility is the law of the Fifth Dimension. It is a pillar of the new societies and the basis of your personal lives. You will awaken in your status as adults.

Growing up can be difficult. However, it is also wonderful to come into one's power and to live one's true potential. Living one's power is vitally important. It is the only way you can fully accept your co-creatorship. Power means developing the necessary safety and self-confidence in yourself in order to take responsibility towards oneself, one's society, and the Earth. This quality will be practiced and integrated by every individual. The resulting societies will take truly extraordinary paths for the good of mankind and for Earth.

The current time of transition into a higher dimension is incredibly intense. It demands that people have plenty of patience and serenity, yet also initiative to let go of the old and outdated in order to make space to create new things.

Your current incarnation on Earth is not coincidental. You are following your souls' plans and motivation. That means returning Light to Earth, and anchoring divine love on Outer Earth again. This motivation has always accompanied you. Now, you will finally be able to harvest the fruits of your extensive efforts, and to abandon yourself to fulfilment safely at the bosom of Mother Earth. Your dreams will come true. A peaceful mankind will pass on into the Light as one.

You will leave all negative influences, fears and nightmares behind. The separation is irrevocable. Take the new path with courage. Try out new strategies. Venture onto unusual paths and re-create yourself. It is truly a rebirth that you are now experiencing. Your personality, your self, will be shaken down to its foundations, in order to be reborn as a new, multidimensional person in a five-dimensional society where unconditional love is deemed the basic matrix.

My dear readers, we will soon approach each other in this unconditional love. We will cautiously approach each other to meet like curious children. Praised be this change of dimension of Outer Earth into the Fifth Dimension. It will bring our long-desired unification. Our hearts are beating faster at the thought. We may still restrain our cheers, but soon the fanfares and trumpets will sound and seal our unification.

First, you will change the fates of your societies from the ground upwards. Love for All-That-Is will enter your communities and allow you to integrate entirely new structures into your political and economic system. The Light impulses that Earth and mankind now integrate have been sparking this process for a long time. The new paradigms developed must adjust to the present vibrational amplitude at any given time. This is an ongoing process that will keep you on your toes in the next few years. A process-oriented global awareness of mankind that will materialise. This is an intense but also very creative time span. The well-being of mankind and Earth will be the main focus. Egotistical goals have no space in this scenario! Since the energy of mankind will be used for the general good, it will be able to generate incredible forces. You will gaze upon the resulting manifestations with pride, and your self-confidence as global mankind will strengthen. A population of Earth, once strengthened in this manner, will then be able to contribute to the cosmic family together with my people, the Agarthans. The cosmic societies of Light have their committees in which they are represented by self-confident, Light-filled beings. They cooperate as partners, i.e. on equal footing. The new representatives of Earth will need, and be able, to contribute as equals in all aspects. The certainty of being embedded into the cosmic societies of Light will strengthen the residents of earth and give them the support for their own processes. Being embedded in a family, no matter if privately or as a human family, is always nurturing and gives the individual stability and strength. Your future human family and the cosmic family of Light are already reflected in your own families. You have wonderful celebrations in your cultures for which you gather as a family. They are incredibly precious opportunities to engage in exchange within the family and to nurture each other in all respects. The private family is also a way to show you how larger societies may work. They can celebrate together, enjoy and forgive. Love is always the basis. Like every Light process must be initiated by individuals, changes to the family structures must originate in the small, private families in order to make larger societies functional. Processes of consciousness always work from the inside outwards. No one will help you on the outside. You will develop your own help from the inside. This will happen through your love for yourself. That is the actual Master's examination that you are currently going through. Our own inner love will automatically make you part of the entirety, the All-That-Is. You will become a goddess/god in action and be able to practice your co-creatorship.

Accepting oneself as one is, finding oneself beautiful and graceful when looking into the mirror, being able to forgive oneself: These are the small signs of loving oneself. Do not forget that our creator is never whole if one of us is missing. We are all part of this wonderful creation. As a consequence, we are all divine. Let us carry our divinity out into the world, and let us bear the responsibility that comes with it.

Your Higher Self is now increasingly merging with yourself. Its radiance will permeate your bodies. Your radiation will first be perceived by your surroundings. It is your purest identification. No amount of make-up in the world will be able to cover it up. Your divine beauty is in this radiance. It will influence your bodies accordingly, healing and strengthening them. The more you are moving towards the Fifth Dimension, the greater your radiance will be. The veil of separation is in the process of dissolving. You will become increasingly aware of the ethereal by seeing, feeling and smelling it. You will perceive wonderful scents when embracing a loved one. You will feel the colours of their aura and feel the love inside them. It's perfectly wonderful, isn't it?

Ecstasy will envelop you when a greater number of people join in meditation or prayer to praise our creator, whose loving radiance permeates all dimensions and can be perceived from afar. They are like manifest pillars of Light that shine into the cosmos and to us into Inner Earth. We always know who we contact and how that person is feeling.

The perception of the ethereal will transform your societies. It will instruct mankind to go to its inner-most self, in order to discover its beauty.

You will admire us and our ethereal bodies with great joy. We, in return, will recognise our beloved family in you, of whom we were separated for so long. Our mutual love will merge and initiate the birth of New Earth. We will continue our journey into the Light in love, and thank our dear home planet Earth for her motherly patience, her incredible beauty and her love for her residents. Together, we will honour Mother Earth and take care of her. We will be grateful to be able to continue our evolution into Light together with her.

Red Crossings

Like your organism, Earth has lines of power that nurture and strengthen the entire system. These lines of power are not only on the surface of Earth. Some cross through the centre, or even just a hemisphere, of Earth.

On the surface of Earth, you are aware of many of those lines of power. Since the ancient times, they have been honoured by your cultures and claimed by them as places of power for their ceremonies. People created their magical monuments, such as pyramids or your cathedrals. Many of those holy sites were built on crossings of these lines of power in order to be able to use the energy present at that convergence. The lines of power on the surface have a great resonance into the inside of Earth, just as the inner lines of power radiate to the surface. Those lines are like pipelines of Earth. She nurtures and energises her surface with them, as well as her inner-most core. That energy is the pure radiance of Gaia, our Earthly Mother. Crossings are where two different lines of her energetic properties meet to build a very powerful field. The lines of power are assigned specific colours based on energy properties. Where two red lines of power cross, they have strong potential properties. They radiate out in all directions, inwards and outwards into the cosmos. When radiation weakens, our star siblings and their suns will recognise this very quickly, reacting to Gaia's call for help in this manner.

Gaia is part of the cosmic family, supported and strengthened by all other stars. After all, it is in the entire cosmos' interest that the journey of her planets goes smoothly. The weakening or failure of one star would have incredibly disastrous consequences for the whole universe. Your many atomic explosions, for example, have severely thrown Gaia out of balance. Only the next generations will become fully aware of these changes. As you are starting to understand, the magnetic resonance has had to find new pathways. The climate changes of the North and South poles are direct consequences of those atomic manipulations. They bring about the corresponding consequences to the climates of their respective hemispheres.

Red crossings are, therefore, very strong in energy and convey plenty of information for their entire environment. They are like energy sources that send their information and quality to Earth, as well as to the cosmos. Stars are living beings that serve as a home to their residents. They also work in a family-like structure, sending their corresponding energies into the adjacent cosmos. The stellar siblings receive the mutual energy and try to harmonise it and to strengthen it at need. Earth travels further and further into the Light together with her solar system and her galaxy. Mutual assistance is, therefore, incredibly important. A great loss of energy in one star would cause the entire community to suffer. The journey could be delayed or even stalled entirely.

As residents of a planet, all are responsible for showing their home planet the love and care that enable it to continue its journey unhindered.

For this reason, I appeal to the love and reason of the people of Outer Earth to show their planet Earth the respect it deserves, for the good of all of us.

Red crossings are places of love, connected to a strong drive and strong potential for manifestation. In such a place, sustainable projects can be implemented and easily put into practice. Start working on your projects with Earth, measuring and sensing their energy. Rigid rational plans will come to fruition less and less, either due to the people living there who have access to Gaia's energy, or through technical prevention that bears clear evidence of the lack of feasibility – the impossibility to fulfil the plans. Listen to and feel the Earth on which you live. You are living in symbiosis with your Mother Earth, your planet. She will provide her wealth to you and support you.

We of Agartha have always worked together with Mother Earth. She has richly endowed us and protected us in return across the eons. We live in conscious symbiosis with her, aware that we are inseparable. We are one. The residents of Outer Earth will soon learn to understand this as well. We are very grateful for this development of conscience, which finally enables us now to show ourselves to Outer Earth and to design life in, and on, Earth in partnership with you. We are aware of your vibrational transformation. We know about your great effort to leave the planet in the healthiest condition possible to the next generations. The more you are moving into the five-dimensional density, the easier such efforts and success will be for you. Do not falter in your work. The well-being of the whole will be the fruit of your efforts. The family of nations will guide you into a terrestrial large family where everyone will take responsibility for themselves and towards the whole. Its roots will reflect its colouring, its characteristics, but its projects will speak of the quality of global terrestrial scales. We are all connected to each other. This is why disasters on one continent can spread their influence around the globe and even impair and influence our territory in Inner Earth. We are one mankind. We have one planet to share as our home. Let us be respectfully and eternally connected to it in love. Hear this wish from your old ancestors of Inner Earth, and heed it. Our gratitude is great. Our love accompanies you.

Earth has many energy lines and places of power. Their energy is acutely present throughout Earth. It is how she promotes her residents, nurtures and supports them. What a wonderful planet we are allowed to live on! Our ancestors have already completed their living and development processes on her. Our ancestors are none other than ourselves, in a different time incarnation. They left their tracks everywhere, both in terms of energy and manifest by buildings. That information of the entire range of Earthen incarnations is here and can be called up by anyone. It is a living library that has stored the progression of conscience. This information reflects your development and clear turn towards the Light of the population of Outer Earth. The processes were tedious, and at times painful.

Now, however, the time has come to write a new chapter of Earth's history. It is a chapter that will unify Outer and Inner Earth in the love and Light of the ONE. Our meeting can only happen in that Light energy, to let our hearts' energy merge into one. What a wonderful future we, and our descendants, are facing! A gigantic potential treasure trove is at our disposal. Our populations will become a unified people of brothers and sisters. As one human family, we will continue our journey into the Light. Soon, all will have their multidimensional potential and use it for the glory of the ONE. Our cooperation will return our planet to full health and allow her to send her radiance into space to match. The interaction with cosmic love will make our populations soar. They will make incredible progress in terms of conscience and spirit, creating their Paradise from Earth. Take the last few steps. Pass the gate to the Fifth Dimension to approach our reunification.

Necessities

In order to cross the five-dimensional gate, you will require the will to transform all the old structures that restrict you. Only this will enable you to encounter the new, the unknown and numinous. It will take courage and trust to find the required certainty and stability within yourself. Achieving that stability is your true task now, along with love for yourself. That love is the quintessence of your further development. It is your true Master's examination. That integrated love will make the steps necessary to radiate your inherent light into your environment easier for you. As a result, it will facilitate change and transformations. You will merge with the high present vibration and let it carry you into a new era of Earth. That energy will take you to your destination. Your contribution will be letting the transformation process happen, and personally stabilising and integrating that high energy level of Light. The evolutionary path of Earth and her people is predetermined. It can only be slowed by personal free will. It is also an individual decision as to whether they want to complete this dimensional change, or prefer to continue to develop further learning processes in a three-dimensional and strongly polarised energy density. Gaia, our dear Mother Earth, will follow her evolutionary path. She will continue to serve as a willing platform for mankind's learning processes, and support them in their personal evolution.

The new era of earth offers entirely new learning processes, from handling of spiritual matter to a harmonised polarity. These are truly new conditions into which you need to grow but that will offer you incredible opportunities. The familiar separation from All-That-Is will be dissolved, and you will become evident as co-creator of your own lives, as well as your own and the cosmic societies.

My dear people, this path is, in the end, your destination in the great, never-ending cosmic game. But only we, the Agarthans, will support you in this process, but so will all societies of Light. Light and love are the motivation of our lives and incarnations. Let us continue on the path of Light towards our shared source, and the ultimate home of our love.

The living processes developed now will free you and continue to carry you up this ladder of ascension. A ladder only has the options of moving forward, staying in place or going backwards. You will choose your path, and the speed at which you take it. You bear sole responsibility for this. This makes your decision for the next step you are taking clear. It will also give you courage and confidence in your own life plan. This ascension into the Fifth Dimension, the adult era, will give you self-confidence and free you from restricting structures. It will seem unbelievable that you have remained fettered to conditionalities for so long, without considering your true selves. Your progress will allow your old self to shed its skin and help give birth to a new person of Light. Welcome your reborn self and stabilise it in this cosmic Light energy. Let those high vibrations stream into every single pore of your bodies and fill them, and your minds, to the brim. Pulsate with All-That-Is and perceive the eternity of being, the connection with above and below. Flow into the prophesied Golden Age of Earth and her residents.

This vibration of love will give you truly great and unique gifts. Explore them and accept your co-creatorship. Create heaven on Earth, your personal – and mankind's - paradise on Earth. The societies of Light inside Earth and in the cosmos will accompany you and rejoice in your path with you. They will praise you for your will and tenacity in following this path of Light. We are proud to continue our journey with Earth together with mankind of Outer Earth. Our hearts are filled with immeasurable love for you. May our vibrations of love touch your hearts. Feel embraced by all of us!

The vibrations of love of the residents of Earth will permeate our beloved home planet, nurture and heal her. Gaia's residents will finally give her the support and love she is due, and her treasures will be available wisely to all. Our Mother Earth will once again be cared for and valued by her human family. Like a loving family, we will continue on our journey into Light and experience new adventures together once united. Our shared history will enrich the cosmic libraries. We have experienced plenty here on Earth. Now, we will open ourselves to the cosmic space. The "Earthlings" will present their treasures and traditions and engage in exchange with the beings of Light in their cosmic neighbourhood. The limits of Earth will be overcome. Existence as an island will be firmly in the past. The future is brimming with possibilities!

Love is the alpha and omega. It is our basic matrix. It is our elixir of life and our future.

From the Inside to the Outside

The spiritual power my people have developed over the course of millennia was targeted at ourselves, but also at Mother Earth. We knew what was about to happen on Outer Earth with its condensed energy, and we strove to provide a counterpoint for Earth and her Outer Residents. The more Outer Earth fell into polarity, the more we strove to stabilise Light in and on Earth. Our Light process anchored Light on Earth. Now, it is reaching the surface. It will merge with your Light process. Earth is ready to experience this energy thrusting outwards all across the globe. The cosmic particles of Light permeate the entire matter of Earth and its ethereal parts, and, of course, also every single one of her residents. This energy will accelerate every single atom. Matter will be spiritualised and acquire five-dimensional qualities. Initially, you will find yourself at a loss for how to handle this quality of matter, which is unknown to you yet. Soon, however, it will enchant you. Spiritualised matter can be modelled with mental powers. It can also be shifted that way. This approach will still seem utopian to you. It will only take a little practice and focus, however, to allow you to work with matter in very unconventional manners. Of course, no-one is born a master. The fascination of handling mental power and matter will, however, leave you enthusiastic and make your access to this easier.

The five-dimensional vibration will be gradually integrated on Earth. This process will take a few decades, or even a few centuries, to come to completion. You are the generations of transition. You are the pioneers who have initiated and designed this dimensional transformation. The following generations will proudly honour you. Their societies will use your achievements as a basis for their own. This energy transformation you are currently going through is gigantic. It implies great transformations of personal and global kinds at the same time. You are ready to build entirely new structures and to adjust them to the five-dimensional vibrational quality. This must be completed before you can create new things in all areas of life. You are living in an incredibly creative era. Your potential and talents will be discovered and used for the greater good. You will find yourself amazed at the projects you will tackle and put into practice in future. The new energy will let you soar. Old inhibitors will disappear. Your co-creatorship will become part of your lives, for the good of mankind and of Earth. This co-creatorship is your birth right, your obligation to the whole, and your natural service on the path of Light.

Many of your achieved innovations will design your societies based on the five-dimensional model. Based on vibrational density, however, you will have to continue to adjust time and time again. Think of it as a brook that develops into a river, and then a stream. Your creativity and innovations will know no longer know any boundaries. Your societies will be fundamentally changed for the good of their people and, of course, Earth. Earth herself will change her face. She, too, transforms in order to absorb and integrate those high vibrations. It is an integrated process that affects the entire planet. Since we already vibrate in the Fifth Dimension, we only experience adjustments here and there. We have avoided greater transformations due to our long Light process, since we were able to integrate our vibrations gradually over the course of centuries. The transition is very intense for us as well. We can feel that our shared vibrational densities are slowly approximating each other. Like the cosmic family, we strive to contact the people of Outer Earth to draw their attention to our civilisation and to strengthen them in their Light process. This Light process will not only benefit you, but also all your neighbours on Earth or in space. We are all eternally connected. We are one great family. As is common in families, the weakest members are strengthened and supported in order to let them become full members of the community. Be assured of our sympathy. We will need Earth as a whole, with all her residents incarnated on and within it, to allow us and the cosmic family to continue the Light process. This is also the reason for our current contact and future unification.

The Light process of the civilisations of Light is unlimited. It will strengthen creation and make it shine. Our creator is expanding!

The internal fire of every individual incites this new wave that will enable us to build an entirely heterogenous society on the planet Earth. The underlying cosmic energy will carry us all and guide us to the new Earth. That new Earth will have nothing in common with the old one. This transition process is often called rebirth for this very reason. It is a birth into a new, five-dimensional Earth, with access to multi-dimensionality. It is a true quantum leap!

From the inside out, it will happen like the eruption of an energetic volcano, but without any danger to people. Quite the contrary: the energy we are sending to the surface of the Earth will merge with the cosmic energy that is being flushed onto Earth. This unification of energies will support you in your Light process and give you the grounding you need. Trust in this Light process. Let it guide and support you and take the steps you need to make your lives more conscious and fulfilled. We are already unified in energy this way. Personal contact will follow suit. As soon as our vibrational amplitudes are compatible, our gates, currently still protected by angels and spirits of Light, will open to you. Soon, we will be able to thank the guardians for their services. They have mastered great and sublime things over all these centuries, and developed their locations into places of power. The locations of our gates will come as no surprise to you as soon as they are disclosed. The gates will soon be activated to be ready to open. Imagine it like the energetic reactivation of a meridian in your bodies. It takes sensitivity and the proper energetic dosage to reactivate such gates. Do not forget that they are part of the body of our planet Earth. Earth is a living being as well. We will proceed with care, in the interest of Earth and her inner and outer residents. The time has come to activate the opening process. We, the populations of Outer and Inner Earth, now need to get to know each other more intimately in order to prepare this step. Mutual curiosity and joy will accompany us and pave our hard path.

Earth is not the only planet with residents inside. Even our solar system knows such facts. Planets or their moons have inner populations, with highly developed civilisations that have set out on the path of Light as well. Maybe, we will encounter them together in the far future.

Excesses Inside and Outside

Exploitations of the resources of Earth is constantly increasing and has driven it close to collapsing. Earth is no longer willing to share what remains of her treasures with mankind. They are vital for her as well, and needed to ensure her survival. This is why your raw material sources will run out. We urgently advise you to rethink your energy strategies. Activate your technology potentials and invest in new energy sources. Human societies will survive with unconventional new technologies that no longer endanger mankind and Earth, but support your activities instead. None of this is new to you. All that is still lagging is implementation. It's like a field that is ploughed anew in order to allow sowing entirely different plants. I understand that you have invested incredible amounts in conventional energy generation, and that a great many people are financially dependent on it. However, there will be no other choice than to embrace new technologies once your current energy generation no longer pays off. The process will have great repercussions on your personal and global lives. Start developing new scenarios in your minds. The time is overdue. Awaken from your trend of growing and wasting and start refining new strategies together with Mother Earth. Invest in new, clean energy generation facilities. Your five-dimensional future will no longer allow you to harm Earth. She, in turn, will support you in your innovative efforts, and show you a new way of producing energy. Take courage, and listen to your inspirations. Put them into practice. This is another path on which Gaia will help you come up with new ideas. Gaia is, as I told you, alive! She is a cosmic being, like you, and like us. Of course, her body and her mission are entirely different from ours, and yet she is also a soul unit. She is a divine being! This awareness will awaken in you as well, step by step, now. Allow Gaia to contact you through your heart and simply enjoy her incredible serenity and beauty. The next generations will develop their paradise here through their many transformations and with the lighter dimensional density. They will find their Garden of Eden, where the "apple" of polarity will be harmonised.

Your achievements will characterise the next generations. They in turn will complete incredible progress in technical and spiritual areas. Each successive generation will contribute in turn to make our planet the home of a happy and fulfilled mankind. After this great transition, the cosmic energy will calm down a little and enable Earth, and her people, to progress at a more leisurely pace on their evolutionary paths. The cosmic Light particles integrated by matter will then need some time to recover a certain stability.

Your inner processes will re-stabilise again. After so many years of transformation, your old structures will have disappeared and given way to new paradigms. Now, you need to face new tasks with a united and freed psyche. You need to look at your lives from the side of the heart and to tackle your human interrelations with love. Your hearts' energy will become the basis for all your commitments, both personal and professional. Your reason will merge with your hearts to enter the multidimensional space, where any connection and project will only be possible based on unconditional love. Multidimensional space will show you that all of us, the terrestrial and cosmic residents, are connected. We were never separated. We have always nurtured and supported each other. The veils of Old Earth will be lifted, and the cosmic splendour will finally be visible to you. It is an energetic fact that will only be possible thanks to your ascension into a higher-vibrational dimension. What a release it will be for the civilisations of Outer Earth, to finally consciously be received into the fold of the cosmic family. Every person had been painfully missing this connection inside, without being aware of its existence. The yearning for the stars has always accompanied you. It found creative entrance into writing, imagery and sound, as well as in your technologies. How liberating is it to finally be able to satisfy this yearning and to feel protected in a greater whole; to powerfully work for this whole and to become a conscious part of this wonderful creation. Love will show you this path, and accompany you. Only love will allow the cosmic contact and the contact with Inner Earth. It is a grand romance of cosmic proportion that will make you ecstatic. It is a romance of superlatives, permeating and nurturing Everyone and Everything. It is an extraordinary vibration that will bring you to new life, new inspirations and new deeds.

The systems of Old Earth have dissolved and given way to the cosmic love in which every individual accompanies and supports the shared fate, fully responsible for their self. What a great future we are all approaching!

Innumerable decades and centuries ago, we were able to welcome the highly spiritual people of the Mayans among us. We have always been connected. We were familiar with each other, and yet their arrival was cause for great celebration. To us, it was one step towards the prophesied, final merging of the populations of Earth. The original people of the Mayans has become integrated well among us, even though they continue to follow their own traditions. The merger with the populations of Earth will follow a similar pattern. All peoples of Earth will be fully integrated on the New Earth, while still preserving their original traditions. This will lead to incredible wealth and exchange among all of mankind. The different peoples base their traditions on the level of their hearts. This makes them suitable for the five-dimensional vibrational level. All egotistical and brutal traditions will stand no chance of survival. They will not be able to cross the gate into this new, high vibration. This is why I speak of wealth. The level of the heart has a great many facets that we can exchange. Some of these facets of the heart will not be common to all people. Yet, it is beautiful and enriching to be informed about them. The peoples will remember their roots and use their potential. The multifaceted population living on Earth reflects the many civilisations of Light in the cosmos on a smaller scale. First, we will become more familiar with each other here on Earth. Then we will set out together into cosmic realms. Outside of Earth, we will develop a strong feeling of cohesion. Our star siblings will perceive us as Earthlings or residents of Earth as a whole, no matter if we hail from Inner or Outer Earth, no matter our continent or ethnicity. Such associations will be of entirely subordinate relevance. Our self-confidence as people of Earth must be strengthened for this, in a process that we will design together in the coming years. We will learn a great amount about ourselves in the course of it. I, and our people, are greatly looking forward to our unification and our exchange with the various peoples of Outer Earth. The high five-dimensional vibration will support this process. It will show all of us that we can merge in a holistic manner on the level of our hearts. Have faith in this process of creation. I know that it must still feel very utopian for you. The cosmic energy now flushed onto Earth will exponentially increase the readiness of all peoples of Earth. This unification is our birth right. Access to the cosmic space will be its consequence. New Earth will truly have little in common with Old Earth. An evolved mankind will be responsible. The separation and fragmentation of peoples and families will have an end. People will see that we are all one in ONE, both on Earth and in the cosmos. This unity will be based on the level of the heart. It will radiate into all traditions and all activities of mankind. An incredible potential of innovations and creative power will be available to us. People will be drawn to the "We", rather than the "I". Family, villages, nations – and all of Earth – will be at the centre. The whole will, in turn, influence even the smallest of cells. It is a give and take on all levels. It will be an exchange of the heart that nurtures and permeates everything. It is key to finding paradise that you have long sought.

Welcome to New Earth with all of its incredible opportunities. Welcome to the multi-dimensional space that contains all of creation, harbours all dimensions and permits conscious access to All-That-Is. It is a great and fundamentally new adventure for mankind of Outer Earth. Together, we will go on a new travel through time with Mother Earth into the cosmic Light. We will explore our galaxy and our universe. Together with the civilisations of Light, we will praise our creator. We are all one. The separation of the people of Outer Earth will be over. That incredible quantum leap gives us immense joy. The quality of our hearts will now merge with yours. Mutual love is our basis and our future. Mother Earth, our home and refuge, will now continue on her journey into the Light with new strength.

Earth – Gaia – Terra

Mankind has given our planet some wonderful names. Her energy is of gentle motherhood and her radiance and physical properties are of incredible beauty. What a blessing it is to be incarnated on this planet, and to be allowed to experience and design the current evolutionary leap. We are all part of a cosmic event that radiates deeply into our universe. It is an event that is welcomed with joy by all the civilisations of Light. It is an event that will strengthen and invigorate all of the universe of Light. Do you understand, now, that I am speaking of a blessing of living here, in and on Earth, to be allowed to go through our learning processes in a dimensional change, and to be able to help design a new cycle?

We will gladly rise to the responsibility that comes with it. After all, we are co-creators of our reality. We are divine sparks in action. We create New Earth for ourselves. We are the captains of our spaceship. Gaia may control the vessel, but we are her crew and her guardians. Together with Earth, we make up a dream team consciously going on their journey, exploring the sky and contributing to the cosmic community of Light. Do you now understand my delight, the joy of my people in being able to finally, consciously implement things together? A great, shared future is waiting for us with Mother Earth. We have a new Earthly cycle to discover! There is an unknown land to be entered and explored! I hope that I have been successful in sharing my enthusiasm with you, to let you abandon your old conditionalities and make such incredible new experiences.

Earth is our home. It has been for eons for some of us, and yet we still need to learn new things from her. the fact that populations are living inside Earth, for example, is such a learning process that has the people of Outer Earth amazed. No matter how far your science has progressed, it remains incomplete concerning the properties of our planet Earth. Her ethereal energies, for example, are usually unknown; yet, they are powerful vibrations that influence great regions. I have already mentioned that Earth is a living creature, nurtured by her chakras like you are. Chakras are ethereal organs that every living being has, nurturing them on an energy level and ensuring their life. The current ascension into the Fifth Dimension will strengthen the various ethereal energy swirls or chakras of Earth since they approximate the cosmic vibrations that surround them. Earth adjusts to this new, high dimension, which brings about changes to her properties. Just as you are changing during this time of ascension, physically and mentally, Earth is also changing to stay involved in this evolutionary process. See the changes in Earth with regards to this, and welcome the process of growth Earth is going through, to grant you the platform for your own evolutionary steps.

Together with Earth, we are growing into this new, multi-dimensional era. We are subject to the corresponding adjustments. Welcome your personal changes, no matter if they are physical or mental. Get ready for a new self. Your new self will transform into a "we". Earth with all her populations will be our focus after all. Now, we will all be caught up in an energetic eddy to carry us all into a new earthly cycle. That new cycle will spiritualise your conduct, as well as the very matter that surrounds you. Your demands will submit to new rules, anchored in your symbiosis in All-That-Is. This new energy cycle will pervade everyone's everyday lives gradually. Its integration will be a process to happen over the course of a few generations. Processes of growth have always been part of your lives. During this dimensional change, they are accelerated and sustainable. Enter this new, high dimension with the necessary serenity and calm, one step at a time. Enjoy the multi-dimensional view it presents to you. Be reborn anew into this new earthly cycle and rejoice in our planet and her civilisations. The cosmic love that connects everything is our basis and our motivation.

Earth as she is perceived is a sphere with land masses and lots of water. Her poles are covered in ice that is melting quickly in the Northern hemisphere, which changes climate accordingly. The Southern pole is rather increasing in ice formation, leading to an imbalance that can have severe consequences for the people of Outer Earth: from climate change, to weather disasters and even axial shifts. The magnetic field of Earth is changing drastically now as well, in order to better allow Earth to absorb the five-dimensional energy. Earth is currently undergoing extreme changes. She is getting ready for the dimensional change, in order to set out on her further cosmic journey together with her solar system.

Earth herself may be a sphere, but inside her, she conceals various Earths that are merged with each other. This merger has created great cavities that produced our habitat. We have a light source similar to your own. We know no nights, since our light source is constant. We also need sleep, of course, in order to regenerate our bodies. The higher energy in which we live, however, makes us a lot more resilient and robust. Our bodies regenerate very quickly. The way we mark time is not comparable to yours. We live in a timeless here and now. The past and future are mired in the present for us. We mark time by various generations. We have been living in a multi-dimensional space for eons, and are intimately familiar with its paradigms. We will gladly share this knowledge with the people of Outer Earth when the time comes.

We rejoice in beautiful landscapes and regions, just as you on Outer Earth do. You would call our climate tropical. We have wonderful blue-green bodies of water and lush vegetation. The quality of our water gives our skins a slightly blue- green sheen as well. Our race is reminiscent of your indigenous Hawaiians or the Maori. We are a very well-protected and healthy people. We do not know your bacterial and viral diseases, which is another reason that may delay our meeting in order to protect us. In the Fifth Dimension, you will increasingly take better care of your bodies. Your immune systems will strengthen, and certain viruses and bacteria will not survive ascension.

As mentioned, we and our habitat have always been vibrating in the Fifth Dimension. Our bodies are less condensed than yours. Let us say that we are somehow more transparent. Your bodies will also reach this status over time. It is caused by the acceleration of your atoms by the current cosmic energies. As mentioned, your long earthly cycle that permeated deeply into matter is now over. It is about to be replaced by a cycle of Light.

After the transfer to the Fifth Dimension, your vibrational amplitude will have to rise to a higher level before we can celebrate our meeting. Our goal can be implemented much faster than you think, since the high five-dimensional vibration will exponentially act on the entire globe and change mankind as a whole.

As you can travel into the cosmos with your body of Light, you can also travel into Inner Earth. Our first contact will be on the spiritual level. Of course, we greatly welcome this. At the moment, it is important that Outer Earth becomes aware of us. You need to overcome your limitations and accept this fact. We understand how difficult it can be for you to let go of such general paradigms in order to embrace new ways of thinking. When Columbus discovered the Americas, the idea people had of Earth had to be changed entirely as it no longer fit with the facts they thought they knew. Do not stand in the way of your own liberation. Allow entirely new models of thought. You will experience such new models of thought not only concerning Inner Earth, but in all areas of your societies and sciences. The thought patterns of the Third and Fourth Dimensions are obsolete. Everyone will have to face the new paradigms and experience great liberation in interacting with matter and all social relationships.

In fact, we are already your future in the Here-and-Now. In a way, we are the anchor of the Fifth Dimension on Earth. At the moment, we are the guardians of New Earth. Go through your transformation processes step by step. We are here, and we will give you the energetic space you need for your adjustments and transformations. We are brothers and sisters of our shared Earth. We will help each other in this important evolutionary step.

This cosmic empathy that will manifest very strongly on Outer Earth in the near future is our motivation and our learning process. Like the cosmic societies of Light, we currently feel responsible for mankind on Outer Earth. Soon, this responsibility will pass back to every single individual. Together, you will then be responsible towards us, but also towards Earth. At that time, there will only be one united terrestrial mankind. Our shared path is pre-determined, and we must follow it step by step. What a wonderful adventure it will be!

Feasibility

The transformations you are currently experiencing in yourself and in your society will create New Earth. A drastic increase of vibrations like the one you are currently going through is forcing you to release old structures in order to allow new models to be born. These new models can only to be implemented after creative introspection. It truly is a process that will return you to humanity, to a higher perspective of cohabitation from man to man, and to Earth. Some groups have always found this philosophy close to their hearts. Now, it will be at the focus around the globe. Egocentric projects will find it hard to prevail in this high energy. Eventually, they will collapse. Projects that have a higher perspective for man and Earth, however, will become established and cause re-education of the population. The financial means for this will be openly provided. The financial markets will be used more and more for the good of everything, since only this will make it possible to use the developed financial liquidity for a profit in future. "For a profit" does not mean the achieved economical profits of Old Earth. That phase has definitely come to an end. You are, after all, moving towards a harmonised polarity that will no longer permit any excess of any kind. That harmonisation will calm down cohabitation on Earth and give you the opportunity to think up and execute innovative projects. What is feasible will become less restrained, without any fear of excess. From a current point of view, it may seem limitless to you. However, never forget that you are entering multi-dimensional space with never-ending opportunities. Gradually, this new habitat will liberate you. You may have to learn to handle the new laws of nature, but their use will amaze you and make your everyday lives much easier. The heavy load will be taken from your shoulders and make you soar.

You will create great things and become conscious co-creators of this New Earth. Your mind will be cleared of the old ballast and your bodies will heal in a holistic manner. By opening yourself to your lives and those of New Earth, you will be able to do great things. Consider the current transformations from this new perspective. It will give you trust and courage to advance on your path into the Light. Mankind reborn from the old dimension will populate New Earth. They will have awakened all the tools of multidimensionality into their bodies and be able to use their entire potential that was developed in many early lives. All the trained talents will be available to them once again. They will wonderfully enrich mankind and Earth. Calm and serenity will restore your incredible potential and enable you to use it in your societies. Dig deep and find the treasures that are locked inside you. With excitement and curiosity, we observe what is in store for you. We are very happy to soon come together in multi-dimensionality and to share our treasures.

What is feasible in your small and large projects depends on your inner attitude. Did you involve your hearts, or are you acting only based on your reason and your solar plexus? You will soon find that the latter is no longer needed. The heart's level will be the basis of your future activities. Your success in this respect will encourage you to stay true to this line of action. Think and create with your hearts. This will include the greater good. You will show respect to Mother Earth. We all develop together with Earth. Egotistical projects are akin to your cancerous tumours. There will be no basis for their existence on New Earth.

It is never good to forget about fun and joy, no matter all the pressure and stress you are under. They are vital for integrating high-vibrational Light particles into your bodies. Your body will become more serene because of this, and better able to handle the energetic adjustment. Your bodies and your minds are preparing for a dimensional change. The corresponding cleansing cannot be avoided. Support your bodies by feeding it, giving it exercise and rest. They are currently doing hard work and need your care. Your care for yourself will bring you into your inner space, where you will find your personal treasure. Given the amount of information that you consume on the outside, it truly is a hard-won skill to get to know and take care of your inner space. You need to deliberately turn away from the outside for this. Believe me when I tell you that your inner treasures will richly compensate you for it, and that you will get to know entirely new aspects of yourselves. This is a great adventure with sustainable effects for yourself and for your environment.

Yes: The level of the heart is the basis for your new projects, no matter if they pertain to your private or professional spheres. Your heart – the organ – is also currently adjusting to the new vibration. It must resolve many old traumas to allow this high energy to better flow through it. The high Light particles draw out all that is negative in order to make space for new energy. Do not be surprised to feel fury and mourning for no apparent reason. Accept it and part with that load. A liberated heart will be able to face new challenges without having old fears catch up with it. Your heart will grow wings, able to engage in any bond without the least prejudice. Such new bonds will happen from heart to heart. The love quotient of a person will be what determines their worth, their wealth. Outer appearances will pale. Yes, I am aware that this is a 180-degree-turn as compared to your current conditions. Since you are moving gradually from the outside to your inner-most, such quantum leaps are only a natural consequence. The next step appears to be a change to your entire civilisations. There will be one human society that vibrates on the level of the heart and takes care of the greater good.

The heart of every individual living in and on Earth radiates the purest energy of love. A hardened heart cannot radiate any energy. It is like a light that has been snuffed out. Those "heart lights" will now be set alight one by one across all the Earth. The cosmic energy that flows in is what causes that ignition. It will invigorate every person's heart. The energy of the heart knows no differences of race, religion or origin! The heart's energy is unconditional and depends on sympathy. It is a multidimensional quality that prevails throughout our universe. That cosmic love is now entering Earth. It will try all structures for their suitability for love. It will transform or eliminate them at need. Every person will experience these processes from the inside out before they will spread through the societies. This process of love will be sustainable. It comes from no specific model of thought or philosophy. Your hearts will be connected to cosmic love and spread it. This is a law of nature of the higher dimension into which you are now growing.

Not all hearts will be able to open themselves to the cosmic love at the same time. Some hearts are wide open already. Others are still fighting change. The higher the vibrational amplitude, the less they will be able to refuse this cosmic love. This fact will produce some chaotic events to come. Trust in this unconditional love that enters you now, to deeply characterise your lives and your societies. Every single heart will eventually be caught up and step in to serve the ONE. The free will of every individual is preserved. Those willing to take this evolutionary step with Earth will open their hearts to this cosmic energy of love.

Earth is moving forward into the light, taking along the people who share her vibration. Earth in turn nurtures her population with this cosmic love. These vibrations of love radiate into your hearts from the cosmos and from Earth alike. It is truly hard to refuse this love!

Our cosmic energy of love is the essence of all lives. It is the cohesive force in our micro- and macrocosm, and our future motivation on our journey into the Light with Mother Earth. Let us accept this cosmic romance and enjoy this energy of the heart that unites us with our creator. Earth will supplement the cosmic chain of Lights and brighten up the universe with the other worlds of Light.

The radiating love energy will measure the feasibility of your projects. The cosmic energy will permeate the new foundations of your structures to ensure their stability.

Progress step by step. Set priorities in your everyday lives. The cosmic energy that is flushed onto Earth now is going to accelerate quickly. If we were in an aeroplane, we would now be told to "fasten our seat belts". Reflect on your next step. Is it targeted at your own development, and the development of the greater whole? Do not forget that only the latter will have sustainable consequences. Stop wasting your time on projects that will only peter out.

Your inner stability is needed now. Become calm and still at intervals, fuel up with energy from Mother Earth. Rooted like a tree, you will be able to weather all the current storms on the inside and outside alike.

In contrast, you will become supports for your families and your environments. Your bodies will transform in order to be able to absorb the new energy. Support it and listen to its needs. It is your manifestation possibility, your divine temple. Your Light potential can shine through it. You are responsible for integrating as much Light as you can into your bodies. Your personal radiance will connect to Mother Earth and the cosmic space. It will contribute to this important evolutionary step. Earth is sprinkled in points of Light. It is an incredible seed that will sprout in the new era, to be harvested by the next generation. A Light-filled mankind will populate Earth and contribute to the cosmic family. The current bearers of Light, the pioneers of the new era, will now be richly rewarded and be able to look at the harvest of their prolonged efforts. Their patience and efforts will have paid off. Earth and her residents will be reborn in a higher vibrational octave and a great step of evolution will be complete.

Mankind is now transforming entirely. The process is reminiscent of the transformation of a chrysalis into a butterfly. Soon, you will be able to use your wings and explore New Earth. Your curiosity will be the driving force of your future adventures. Let them surprise you and enjoy New Earth to the fullest. Playful interaction with her will leave you unchanged. Like a butterfly flies from blossom to blossom, you will find the nectar in your area of activity and enjoy fulfilment.

The high energy will show you what is feasible. Innovative ideas will open up new paths for you.

Only those of the important goals you have set for yourself that support the whole in a sustainable manner will survive the dimensional change. A paradigm change is being prepared. It is already visible here and there. This is a time of tradition with accelerated energy that cannot be evenly integrated in all places. You need to adjust your projects to the current level of feasibility and add the corresponding corrections as energy increases. Only this will give your projects a solid and sustainable structure that can grow into the new era and serve you and the whole. Be prepared for changes and proceed step by step into the new era. This period of time demands plenty of flexibility and improvisation from you. Some of your will have great issues with this, while others will see this scenario in a more relaxed manner. All, however, will experience a time of great change. The old will disappear while the new is not yet in sight. This will greatly challenge your stability. Your environment will provide less and less orientation. Your current learning process is the search for your real self. It truly is a quantum leap that forces you to look inwardly, and to seek and find your personal stability in your being. Outer authorities will no longer be able to manipulate and bully you. You are responsible for yourself on this Earth, with all the consequences this entails.

The accelerated energy will support you in your personal process and continually increase clarity for you. The current change into a multi-dimensional existence is a novelty for Earth and its Outer Population. Everyone must tackle these learning steps on their own and integrate them. You are masters of your path. You can only subject yourselves to this initiation. This will culminate in a responsible society that can progress into cosmic realms while firmly anchored on Earth. Responsibility for the whole is the new prerequisite that forms the basis for your cosmic cooperation. With this integrated principle, new technologies will be provided to you in order to revolutionise your lives on Earth in all respects. You can see that the work to be done is concealed in every single individual. Start your internal journey and be surprised by your own universe. Strengthened from the inside out, you will make the impossible possible and fully live your co-creatorship. The people of Outer Earth will grow up now and are fully responsible for both the whole and their selves. Soon, we will be able to meet and engage in exchange on the same plane. We of Agartha can hardly wait for that time to come. We are greatly looking forward to tackling the fate of Earth together with you soon, and to introduce ourselves in cosmic space as one Earthly family as we actively work for the good of the family of Light.

Our cosmic family has always viewed us as one Earthly family. Our conscious unification is part of the evolutionary step that Earth and her populations are now taking. Our approximation is a process that will take some time. It is the maturation of the degree of conscience of every resident of earth that will achieve this unification. Many smaller and larger steps will be necessary to better get to know each other, and to give any fears or irrational occurrences no opportunity to manifest. This process should grow as naturally as possible in order to turn our unification into a celebration for the entire population of Earth. The extreme acceleration of the current energy will catapult the people of Outer Earth into a multi-dimensional vibrational octave and trigger many learning processes in every single individual. This energetic adjustment of every individual will till the soil for our meeting. Current lack of understanding will dissolve to a great extent. The population of Outer Earth is about to complete an incredible quantum leap in its development. This quantum leap will enable you to welcome outer realities of life, both on Earth and in the cosmos, and to deal with them as partners.

My dear people, you will think and act in different ways than you are used to. Old habits of human societies will be obsolete. New actions that include loving and unifying aspects will become the order of the day. This quantum leap will let you finally overcome all that separates you. You will be able to accept yourselves as cosmic citizens. Our projects will be founded on a loving and unifying basis. They will be aligned not only globally, but even cosmically. The island existence of Outer Mankind of Earth is over. An entirely new, brightly shining adventure is in store for you. It will let you merge with All-That-Is. Love will become the supporting force of your new life, connect you with everything and support you. Conscious responsibility of your co-creatorship will guide you and the coming generations into the "Golden Age" of Earth. Your spiritual and mental wealth will nurture the other cosmic civilisations and they will share their own wealth with you in return. After all, we are one divine family.

The Path of Light

Light displaces darkness. It dissolves it and allows clarity to spread. This happens on both personal and global levels. This clarity is an important part of the process of ascension, new structures cannot be built on uneven ground shrouded in mist. Just look at the current scandals and discoveries in this context. The multi-dimensional era you are growing into has a never-ending perspective where nothing can be concealed or covered up. Complete openness and transparency will be required in all of your enterprises in order to create a stable basis for your new societies. We are all cosmic citizens and, as a consequence, connected in the ONE. We all are co-creators of our reality, from the smallest cell to the size of the very universe itself. Such a co-creatorship can only be created on solid ground, with knowledge of all the different facets. All is interwoven with everything in a fabric of Light that has no gaps or holes. As soon as you enter the multi-dimensional terrain and develop a way to handle these new vibrations, it will become a matter of course for you. The current cleaning phase is preparing that new era. It will also test everyone's responsibility for their compatibility with the energy of the heart that is now becoming established. Love is this Light that is now flushed onto Earth to transforms your hearts. Your hearts will absorb this Light in themselves and radiate in your body like little suns. Your sun-like emanations are cosmic love, filling the entire planet and embracing her residents. These skills of yours will now spread gradually. Old structures will fall apart because they no longer have anything to oppose this energy of love. Old laws that are missing love will dissolve. Your shoulders will be relieved of their burdens as you are approaching a great liberation. Yes, one can say metaphorically that you will come into your wings and view the world from an entirely different perspective. This multi-dimensional perspective will challenge you. You will design innovative creations from your inner selves. Remember, the entire potential that is stored in your DNA will be available to you. Things you learned in other incarnations will be available to you. Time is an illusion, and everything is present in the Here-and-Now. You will recover access to parallel worlds to contribute your past talents to your current lives. This is an exciting and fascinating time that you can now design on Earth. A great range of talents will now be manifested through your bodies. The high vibration automatically filters out negative former talents. Only manifestations that are aligned multidimensionally and carried by the energy of love will find their way into the new era of Earth. There will be no need for you to curb yourself.

Disagreements and issues will come to unusual solutions. At times, you will feel as if you are breaking through the wall of sound that limited your abilities. Interestingly, it will feel entirely natural to you. This is how you can recognise the new energy in your actions. These new solution approaches can also be found on the global stage. They will multiply in future and can characterise your everyday affairs in politics and society. Facts that used to be impossible to change will start to sway and transform. Societies you consider totalitarian and partially backwards will open up to this new, high energy, and contribute their share to a positive future of human civilisation.

These transformations and, at times, even quantum leaps, will happen in just a few years. The cosmic energy of love will reach the hearts of people, no matter if they are living in successful democracies or in totalitarian states. The human potential for love is universal and will break through all barriers of society. Separation is a quality of the Third Dimension. It will be unable to survive in the new five-dimensional vibration. Understanding of the unity with All-That-Is will be revealed to your hearts, find its way into your societies, and transform them accordingly. This change will be welcome. After all, it means adjustment to the deepest yearnings of your hearts. Your societies will change from heart to heart. Every individual will first transform themselves. Their new energy will then stream into their environment and their society. This inner process is what will change everything, forming a basis for sustainable new structures. As I have mentioned before, it is neither a model of thought nor a philosophy. It is the deep desire of your hearts that will change life together on Earth. Your inner self will create and implement all of your decisions. No outwards authority will be able to prune your potential or manipulate you anymore. Every person will be responsible, and every person will be connected to All-That-Is. It is a great, living network of cosmic citizens that invigorate and strengthen our universe.

Unification with the residents of Inner Earth, as well as with our star siblings, is our most natural future. It will be a give and take in a loving new era. It will be an exchange on the level of the heart. The residents of Earth have chosen the path of Light, the cosmic romance. The time has now come, and the gate into that higher octave of vibration has opened. The pull of Light has already enveloped and embraced you. You are crossing the gate to your true and divine destination: To yourself. Welcome to New Earth. Welcome home.

The path of Light is your future. It will offer you entirely new options. The dark, starkly polarised past will soon be over thanks to your willingness to change. You are lined up to start the race. You are still in the process of shaking off the old energy, in order to set out on new paths free from old ballast. Those new paths must be felt and sensed. They are no longer determined by your reason alone, but have become an integrated matter. You will need all of your senses now. Passion, cheerfulness and joy will be your companions from here onwards. The latter qualities are of great importance. The path of Light has nothing to do with severity, hardship and mortification. It is based on prosperity and joy. Let the high cosmic vibrations of love carry you and enjoy them in full. There is enough energy for everyone. The more you integrate that energy into your bodies, the more energy you will have available. Do not deny yourself. Do not forego it, but drink in as much of this energy as you wish. The more of this wonderful energy you can integrate into your bodies and minds, the greater your multi-dimensional share will be. It will allow you to better manifest your co-creatorship as a result.

In order to accelerate this process, you need to change your own manner of thinking. Trust in this new model. You are not taking away from anyone. Quite the opposite! By integration of the high Light particles you will help yourselves, but also all of Earth. The more Light particles are integrated on Earth, the faster will we all move on our shared path of Light.

Throughout Earth, these high Light particles are integrated into man and matter. You are progressing towards spiritualisation of matter. It will become easier to handle. Adjustment processes are a matter of course. The new, creative options will make you enthusiastic and entice you to try out passionate projects. It will likely be the most creative time the residents of Outer Earth have ever experienced.

Border-crossing gadgets of an entirely new scope will appear in all human matters. Earth will once again become a playground for mankind. After all, the people have decided to take the path of Light in their symbiosis with Mother Earth. The new learning processes will take place in an atmosphere of harmonised polarity, without borders and full of joy, always in harmony with the cosmic energy of love. What a new world view it will be for mankind! The path of Light is floating in different spheres. The dense heaviness of your past is entirely unknown to it.

Tangibility

The tangible is in the high energy that is now flushed onto Earth. That energy will change your societal structures in all aspects. It will bring your inner-most to the surface. Many old conditionalities will collapse or undergo most pervasive transformations. This process of transformation will enter all areas of being. It has a global character. Every individual and every human society will be affected by it, able to ready themselves for the new era. This transformation, or rather: this rebirth of Earth with her civilisations, will create the space for the high-quality energy that it is due. Spiritualisation of all matter on Earth is underway. Earth as a whole is entering the Fifth Dimension. That level has nothing in common with Old Earth. It is the gateway to the higher dimensions, to the multi-dimensional space that is present throughout the cosmos. Everyday life will, of course, change severely for the people. During this time of unrest, your love for yourselves and for the whole will be the stable factor. Your relationship to yourself, calm and stillness, are of the utmost importance in this transition. They give you the stability you need to wisely proceed along your path and to tackle many new learning and living processes. This will likely be one of the most learning-intensive times in human history. You will have to learn from the very basics how to handle spiritualised matter, using entirely new personal behavioural patterns. A mind cleared of your old ballast will undergo an incredible opening process and open itself to multi-dimensional experience. Restrictions are only memory. The cosmos will be wide open for new, unlimited excursions of your creativity and imagination. The manifestation of this creative expression is the logical implementation of this incredible process. Humans will become conscious co-creators of their realities. Human civilisations will undergo pervasive restructuring and new living platforms. As mentioned already, this will affect all human societies. Some will be changed more and others less, depending on the progression of the respective status of their consciousness. Personal growth of every individual will be decisive. Every person will be fully responsible for this process. Human societies are renewing themselves from the inside out. External authority will no longer be accepted. Therefore, this time is not a revolution, but a rebirth into a new level of existence, where everything has to be learned and discovered anew. An incredible adventure is waiting for you, and will let you conquer it with all your senses.

The tangible is just ahead and all around you. Every person was born into a social environment that enables them to use their talents in combination with the new, high energy. The search commences in yourselves. It will then spread into your environment with global and cosmic effects. Each of your developments will affect the whole. The quality of three- and four-dimensional separation is over for good. You will become increasingly aware of your connection to All-That-Is. This will let you mature into responsible cosmic citizens. Your thoughts, which will be the basis for your future projects, will produce humble and respectful implementations intended to benefit everyone. Harmonised polarities will let your thoughts run on an energetic middle ground. Negative thought excesses are no longer compatible with the new cosmic energy. They will not live to see the transfer to the higher octave of existence. The more Light particles you are able to integrate in yourselves, the more quickly the five-dimensional realities will become part of your everyday lives. Every person will integrate those Light particles in their own manner and at their own speed. This will even lead to discrepancies in their interactions with their environments at times. I greatly recommend withdrawing to one's own self in that situation. This will strengthen and stabilise you. The transfer to the following vibrational octave is an individual, conscious step. Everyone is their own master and initiates it on their own. This is why external authorities will no longer have any access to this intimate, personal zone of consciousness. Recognise yourselves and become masters of your lives.

This integrated personal process will, of course, affect your lifestyles of your societies. You will construct five-dimensional living spaces with the matching social and political structures. New societies will adjust to their people and support them. Power will be spread among all people. Self-responsibility is connected to taking over one's personal power. Being empowered means being grounded, centred, and responsibly contributing to the greater whole.

Your work will be born from new energy and already have higher dimensional qualities. Since your awareness adjusts to this high energy gradually, destructive projects are increasingly impossible. As I have explained, this evolutionary step is an individual one. There will always be people who refuse admission to the new, high energy. In the long run, refusal of that energy will become impossible. Body and mind of all people will have to adjust to the common energy amplitude in order to survive. As you can see, it is only a matter of time until all people living on Outer Earth will integrate this cosmic energy. Be a little more patient. New Earth is almost close enough to touch. It is certainly close enough to see! A time of transition is always connected to chaotic unrest.

Understand this from a higher perspective, and actively work to design New Earth.

Expansion of your points of view into multi-dimensional spaces must be lived and experienced with all senses. It is a new platform of life that is revealing itself to you now and that needs to be explored. Learn the new facts of life and build your daily lives and your futures on them.

A time of truly unlimited creativity is up ahead, waiting to be conquered by you. Model your here-and-now with your thoughts and give it space to manifest. The high energy will let your ideas convert into reality faster than ever. Be greatly aware of your thoughts and wishes. You must learn and try your hand at the handling of such high energy. New laws of matter need to be considered. Matter has integrated many Light particles and become spiritualised. The new way of handling matter will astonish you. Difficulty, and all that is tedious, will be strongly reduced. Look forward to a time of spiritual manifestations, of steering and modelling this new matter. This, too, will take learning to be implemented in connection with your increase of conscience. You are divine co-creators on your level of existence. You will now be provided with the multi-dimensional pallet. Use this divine gift generously. There is enough for everyone! All civilisations of Light use this cosmic wealth and create their own needs. There will be no limits to your ideas. What you desire will be much easier and simpler to implement. Gradual recognition of yourself will turn your wishes and thoughts increasingly towards a five-dimensional quality, helping you manifest and implement your ideas. The farther you ascend on the evolutionary ladder, the more sustainable and simple your wishes and visions will be. This conscious work is already part of your everyday lives. It will continue in the new octave of being. All five-dimensional thought models already in existence will still be able to realise their full scope. The "soil" will be tilled for them.

Of the Endless Expanse of the Human Consciousness

Your consciousness used to be bound in the three- and four-dimensional level of existence. Great training or certain drugs were needed to experience border-crossing experiences of consciousness. The energetic lift of Earth will now finally open the gates into the never-ending vastness of consciousness. This process will unfold step by step, based on the current amplitude of Earth. Your mind and bodies will be able to get used to the new situation. Therefore, you will not have to fear any mental short-circuits. Like all experiences of consciousness, the new high energy will also require the corresponding training as its basis. Exploration of the mental/spiritual spaces must be tackled with consideration, and requires a good connection back to Mother Earth. This grounding will give you the stability you need to enter high-dimensional spaces while still staying firmly anchored in your Here-and-Now lives on Earth. The fundamental essence is your life on Earth, which is shone on, and shot through, by mental/spiritual energy. The yearning for mental/spiritual experience will strongly increase in the new octave of being. An increase of integrated Light particles will not only spiritualise matter, but also your spiritual needs. The merger with All-That-Is will permeate your bodies and minds deeply. Yearning for connection of all kinds is strong, so too will your curiosity to break out of your island existence. Mental/spiritual cosmic journeys, as well as spiritual contact with my people of the Agarthans, will cease to be unusual.

We are greatly looking forward to contacting you, and to share our joint love with Mother Earth. All of these connections will be the basis for later personal contact, either on Earth or in cosmic space. The love to creation will guide and connect us all. The fruits of this mutual love will flow into your personal lives and enrich them. Incredible wealth will be developed by your mental/spiritual yearning. This will be a wealth that will give your civilisations a gigantic evolutionary push in all respects. The rise to a higher dimensional octave will affect every single atom. Your soul-selves will now unite with your bodies. The separation is in the past. The amplitudes of your bodies will finally permit unification. This symbiosis of your new self will then determine your everyday lives and your path through life as a whole. Great deviations from your path to date are possible, and even probable.

Your mental/spiritual development will change. Access to the eternal cosmic vastness will dissolve many of your limiting paradigms. You will become a cosmic citizen, subject to different paradigms than you are used to from your societies, step by step. You will be confronted with a cosmic, unconditional love and compassion for all of creation. These are qualities that you often cannot find on Earth. Such qualities, once integrated in a person, will initiate incredible changes. I am certain that you understand this.

Your societies will adjust to the cosmic civilisations. These changes will contribute to mankind of Outer Earth renewing from the inside and adjusting to the cosmic civilisations of Light. This development will enable you to connect to the populations of Inner Earth, as well as the cosmic civilisations. This, in turn, will bring an incredible evolutionary push in all respects for the people of Outer Earth. As you can see, your development will start in yourselves. It is a mental/spiritual path that will guide mankind into multi-dimensional spaces. Future scientists will receive their ideas and inspirations from such spaces, manifesting them on Earth. A scientist must, therefore, develop mentally/spiritually in order to acquire such information. Their tools and their professional competency will allow them to implement such innovative ideas here on Earth. They will benefit the greater good in this way. Your mental/spiritual development will be the basis for a new society. It will rest on unconditional cosmic love and compassion for all of creation. The people on Earth will become a conscious part of the cosmic family, connecting to All-That-Is. All facets of love will be reactivated. They will entirely embrace the globe. All of your religions will be reduced to love. Only love has a connecting effect. Love is, after all, the basis for all religions. All separating structures will dissolve. They are rendered irrelevant. Every culture has its own access to creation with its special rituals. Love for our shared creator connects us, rather than separates us. Such love is a matter of the heart. It comes from the inside. Outer authorities will no longer be welcome. Every person will take responsibility, acting from the inside out. Limiting structures no longer have any space in such a world. All that separates, destroys. It will not live to see the high amplitude of New Earth. Love is the energy that binds everything on, and in, Earth, and in the cosmos. We are all forever lovingly connected to each other. Mankind of Outer Earth is only now learning this.

Quantum leaps in your manner of thinking and action are ahead. You are showing the first indications of becoming ready for this. However, some fundamental structures still need to be transformed to fully and entirely manifest you in this new energy. Such changes are processes in which mankind must keep up with the accelerated energy in order to put together sustainable innovations. For now, the most important thing is integrating that high energy in every individual. You will feel the need to change in this respect. The first changes will happen in your personal area. From there, they will take a hold of entire societies. Be prepared for great restructuring. The changed living contents and goals will return greater rest and serenity to people, and show them what being human actually means. Each tradition will find its own approach and its own implementation strategies. This is a good thing. The global citizen of Earth will not become uniform. They will preserve their typical, traditional attributes. This is also a treasure of mankind that should be preserved. Like the cosmic civilisations differ greatly, in more than merely their physical shapes, but also in their own principles of life, we here on Inner and Outer Earth comprise populations of different races and languages. Cosmic love connects all of these hearts. It is the divine sustenance that makes our coexistence possible. It shows us our shared path. Let us take this path together as citizens of Earth, to enable us to join the cosmic family. This may be all new for the residents of Outer Earth. Rely on our experience. Only if all civilisations of Light work together will we be able to continue on our path and our further cosmic journey with Mother Earth on our path of evolution. Our creator represents unity in love, the source and motivation of all of our incarnations, and our goal. Love holds all of creation together. It is its heartbeat and breath. Life without such love only means survival. It has no chances of success. The paradigm of separation dissolves now. We all continue united on our path into light towards our divine destiny. May divine love fill your hearts now, and enliven them after this long time of abstinence. Become what you have always been: divine co-creators of your own realities.

The Implementation of Your Wishes

Your thoughts will manifest faster as the Earth energetically accelerates. This leads to responsible control of your thoughts and wishes. Targeted wishing thoughts that serve the whole already have great manifestation opportunities. The more the new energy is integrated in you, the better you will be able to creatively put your thoughts into practice. You are divine co-creators. This will enable you to bundle your ideas and thoughts for manifestation. Think your plans through to the last detail, and give them the opportunity to become real. I ask you to be emotionally involved in this process as well. Your new creations are integrated, both for yourself and for the whole. As mentioned, strictly egotistical wishes that do not serve the whole will no longer have any factor of fulfilment. The new era will be primarily about the good of the whole. Personal wishes that include this stand a good chance of becoming real.

Control of your thoughts is now increasing in importance. Your thoughts are part of you. They are to support you, rather than proliferating freely. The world of your thoughts should become disciplined, rather than enjoying any life of their own without your influence. Your entire personality is subject to you. You bear full responsibility for yourselves. Do not allow parts of your personality to run away from you and develop lives of their own. You are only strong as your whole self. Only this perspective will enable you to bear full responsibly for yourselves. Bundle the various parts of your personality into a strong self. This – your – strength will be in great in the times ahead, in order to tackle all changes. Strength in a society always begins with the individual. Only this way can sustainable decisions be put into practice. This means that you need to strive to live as consciously as you can. Letting yourself go and being dragged along has no place in the new time. You are the captain of your personalities and your lives. You bear full responsibility. You need to question situations in life and verify that they match you. Surely, it will take courage at first to break out of certain living situations and to take your own path. The high energy will only allow you authentic, conscious paths in life. Many people will now be able to powerfully walk their own paths.

Authentic, conscious paths in life require clear access to oneself. One must accept one's talents and benefits, but also one's dark sides, and try to transform the latter. Transformed downsides can become your most important tools towards a better design of your lives. Accepting yourself is the love you feel for yourself. That love is becoming more and more important. The new octave of being will be conquered from the heart. Without any love for oneself, love for others and for Earth will prove difficult. Love for yourselves and your own universe will radiate through you and touch your surroundings. Serenity and well-being will be perceived by your contacts, who will, in turn, be able to recognise those qualities in themselves. Love for yourself has a contagious effect, as well as a liberating one. The people you interact with will no longer be overwhelmed, and can dispense with any protective mechanisms. Simply being, with all one's strengths and weaknesses, truly is a great quality that will dissolve a great many of your interpersonal issues.

This path of love to oneself requires a stillness and calm. You must turn away from the outside and towards your inner-most self, where all your treasures are waiting for you. Your journey to yourselves will outshine all external activities. It will probably be the most exciting adventure of your lives. Everyone has their own method to find themselves. Every personal approach is the right one. You are divine co-creators. In your inner-most self, you will find your own divinity. After this long time of separation, it will once again shine in your everyday lives. Implementation of your wishes will then contain your divine essence and contribute to the good of everything. Love, and the journey of people to themselves, will allow you to discover your divinity. The connection to your own divinity is the basis of the "Golden Age" and a great step on your evolutionary path. The Gods of Earth will engage in exchange with the Gods of the heavens and merge with them in order to come closer and closer to their creator on their journey into Light.

Many new and innovative ideas and wishes will now reach you through this high energy. Projects that were impossible to implement before now reach the realm of the feasible. Your thoughts and wishes are energies that manifest. Send them out with caution and consideration to make sure that they serve you and the whole. Incredible creations will appear in the near future. They will simplify your everyday lives and improve your living quality. Complicated interrelations will become simpler and better structured. Dependencies will dissolve, since every individual is fully responsible. This requires them to keep an overview of their lives. Dependencies of all kinds are no longer compatible with this new energy. This is why such scenarios are now dissolving. A new awareness of responsibility will take that place, allowing mankind to live more consciously. This responsibility must, of course, be learned first. Believe me: it will have an incredibly liberating effect on your lives. Handling of that new freedom must, of course, also be learned and experienced. This must be a wonderful new experience, a new adventure, to enrich your lives. Liberty is limited only where it impairs the well-being of the greater whole. You must adhere to this one standard. The new energy will bring unconditional cosmic love and cosmic compassion to Earth with it. Egotistical tendencies will be obsolete. The high energy will help you and support you. The old stresses, confusions and quarrels are over. Innovative ideas and wishes will now find the space to come true. You are setting out into a new octave of being, fully of creative opportunities and their realistic implementation. Your creativity will grow wings and soar, lifting you out of your limiting perspectives into free, untouched spaces. This is the cosmic gift of this high energy to the humans of Outer Earth.

Purposeful Actions

I have talked a lot about your new responsibility and the change of mankind into the status of adults. This change now leads to responsible handling of yourselves, but also in the manner in which you contribute to your societies. The new communication can no longer bear any vertical discussion elements. It will only happen from the position of partners. All incarnated souls have chosen their place on Earth in order to serve themselves and the greater whole. They act from their positions and pass on their impressions in this respect. All others must respect them. Every person is aware of their respect and will be treated with respect themselves. Differences of class, race and status will disappear. Every person will design their own lives consciously from their existence, and contribute to the well-being of the whole. This change to people's acceptance will be brought about by the high energy and bring with it incredible human treasures. In the past, many people have been unable to contribute to society without reservations, since they would have suffered painful consequences from doing so. Being human is greatly multi-faceted! Those many facets now bring about many bright hues and the corresponding enjoyment of life. Everyone will design their own projects and activities purposefully for themselves. The societies of Outer Earth will find this conceals an unknown creative potential that will activate all your senses and improve your enjoyment of life. This high energy will increase your purpose in life, but also your fully-utilised enjoyment.

By purposeful action, I mean bundling your creative ideas into a goal that can be realised. Dissolution of your limitations will provide you with a multi-dimensional choice. It may be confusing at first. Explore your new territory in small steps. Feel, smell, sniff and try it all out! Over time, you will find what is suitable for your project. Afterwards, you can use your new resources specifically for your work. Like an artist designs their pictures with their pallet of paints, you will approach and feel your projects. All of your senses will be needed in figure in order to get the greatest possible benefit from this new treasure. That treasure belongs to everyone. It is available to everyone. You will find new colours and shades there, and a new way of handling spiritual matter. You will learn new interaction with harmonised polarity. These changes and innovations are about to manifest, step by step, to match the amplitude of Earth. Integration of the cosmic Light particles will not cease. It will considerably change your everyday lives. This is great news. They should make your heart beat faster in joy!

You are about to break out of your three-dimensional prison and experience access to multi-dimensionality through ascension into the Fifth Dimension. What a blessing it is to be allowed to experience and help design such an incredible time span on Earth!

The many pending, or already completed, changes have greatly challenged you, and will continue to do so. They can be personal or global. Obsolete structures can no longer be integrated into the energy of New Earth. They must either be strongly transformed, or entirely dropped. Of course, this will lead to unrest and chaos. However, creative adjustment to New Earth and its societies will follow as well. Those societies will renew themselves from the inside out. Their respective traditions will be adjusted to the high energy, putting the individual at the focus. This way, every person will receive the respect they are due. They will be able to fully and consciously work for themselves and the whole as citizens of Earth. The high energy will guide mankind in their decisions and involve global responsibility. Every single person will become fully aware of their responsibility for Mother Earth and handling her as their provider. People will learn to treat Earth as a partner for the good of the greater whole. When I speak of the greater whole, this is, of course, not only referring to Earth, but to the entire cosmos. We are all connected to each other. We all bear this great responsibility together.

All of evolution will be affected if a planet does not subject to the whole. It is similar to your cancers. Every cell – or every planet as the case may be – is obligated to the entire universe. Only this can permit sustainable growth on an evolutionary path. This understanding is still new for the people of Outer Earth. As energy continues to accelerate and the new paradigms resulting from it become established, however, it will become clear to everyone.

This high energy that the cosmos now flushes onto Earth is the information of cosmic love and cosmic compassion. They penetrate matter into every single atom and transform every person into a five-dimensional citizen. The many changes are really only energetic adjustments with the corresponding personal and global consequences. The need for change is omnipresent among all people. It is nothing but the logical consequence of this energetic ascension into a higher octave of being. This high cosmic vibration not only raises up Earth and her residents, but our entire solar system and our Milky Way. A cosmic project is now taking place on Earth. We are all connected to each other and will take a great step forward on our path into the Light.

Liberation from your island thinking towards a communal cosmic philosophy is being implemented right now. It will change mankind's deepest beliefs and knowledge of reality. It truly is the greatest transformation that Earth and her residents have ever seen. The time of shadows is over. We will all walk into the Light of our creator together, enjoying their presence in All-That-Is. As co-creators in our reality, we carry the cosmic game into our everyday lives and our societies, to transform Earth into our paradise. This is both our birth right and our cosmic obligation. We are all part of the cosmic family. We are part of creation!

In order to avoid any torturous detours during this time characterised by great change, specific projection followed by action to the same purpose are vital. Since change always brings about unrest, sustainable reflection on your projects is important. Consider the many options available to you, then choose the most sustainable solution for your projects. Consider the possibility of future adjustments that may become necessary at intervals, due to the increasing acceleration of energy. Therefore, try for the broadest possible base for your plans to keep them compatible with adjustments. That way, you can minimise time and resources and avoid chaotic situations.

During these days, developing stability is often difficult. Every individual must tackle and integrate this personally. It is likely going to be one of the great trials of mankind. Everyone will find this stability in themselves, and with Mother Earth. A good grounding with Earth will not only show you her love, but also make you strong and ready to withstand any storm. It is comparable to the roots of a tree. The better a tree is rooted in the soil, the better it will be nurtured and able to survive storms. This access to Mother Earth is integrated and will be achieved through all your senses.

We, the Agarthans, maintain a very special connection to Earth. She is our First Mother and our provider. We want to introduce you to our love for her and show you the symbiosis we all have with her. That way, you can learn to value her manner again and continue on your journey into Light with her with gratitude.

Our love for Mother Earth will consciously connect us once again. It will point us our further shared path for our journey. Well-being of Earth is existentially vital for all of us. It is the only way into our future. May the people of Outer Earth recover their loving connection to Mother Earth, and may they soon cease to exploit her. Respect and love for Earth are qualities that mankind of Outer Earth would be well advised to develop. Exploitation of all kinds will affect the following generations, causing severe hardship for them. Try leaving an Earth worth living on behind for your future generations. Restrict yourselves as necessary for it now. Mother Earth will richly reward you for it and give you the paradise you dream of. Let her act freely and enjoy her sweet fruits. Rejoice in her breathtaking beauty, and open your hearts to her unique energy.

My heart feels drunk with her beauty and her energy of love. May these sparks of the heart reach your hearts and ignite the fire there, too.

Eyes of a Seer

Your eyes let you perceive the wonderful beauty of Mother Earth, your loved ones, and your environment. Sometimes, your eyes must also perceive pain, horror, and ugly things. These perceptions penetrate deeply into your being, to bring you joy or pain. Your eyes are strongly connected to your reason. In part, they integrate holistic access to the world around you, but you need more than just your eyes to acquire holistic sight. It takes the heart, the hands and feet, and the skin as well. In other words, it takes all of your senses. Your entire person perceives life on Earth and should contribute accordingly. The more the high cosmic energy will be integrated, the better you will be able to perceive life on Earth with all your senses. You will even acquire extraplanetary and innerterrestrial impressions. Our eyes are an extraordinary gift from our creator and will receive an even more amazing characteristic, a holistic view of things, through our senses.

Your Third Eye will let you perceive the depths of yourself and your environment. The combination of these different perceptions will give you X-ray vision with just a little practice. You will be able to look beyond the veil – behind the staged front – of a person or an event, and perceive your object in a holistic manner. The information acquired from this will be a great help for your relationships and your projects.

The better the high energy now integrates on Earth, the easier it will be to view new territories and events. At times, you may feel as if you are suddenly seeing Light. Facts that you were unable to perceive with your three-dimensional eyes will reveal themselves to you. They will naturally give you a new understanding of your reality. Your entire bodies are adapting to the new, high five-dimensional vibration. You will become cosmic co-creators. Your bodies will be given the multi-dimensional tools this takes. Your view of things will change as holistic perception becomes possible. You will truly feel as if you had been stumbling around in the dark so far, when suddenly you are given the gift of Light. That metaphor may seem excessive to you, but wait and see. Let developments surprise you! Learn to see, rather than to merely look. A seer will see with all their organs and senses. It is an integrated way of experiencing life on Earth and the co-inhabitants on it. Seeing persons are supported and guided by the energy of their hearts. Looking ones, in contrast, are influenced by their reason. They cannot comprehend comprehensive and sustainable conclusions. You are now in the process of turning from looking to seeing. Do not be afraid if you are suddenly perceiving more than usual. Be grateful that your body is adjusting so well to this high energy instead.

Integration of the high cosmic energy is now at the focus of every resident of Earth. Everyone has to focus on their bodies and try to integrate these high Light particles. Integrating new things, however, requires a certain cleansing from old, outdated patterns and structures. Letting go of old ballast is a process that you are currently busy with, and that will keep you busy for the near future. Have courage and stand by yourselves without compromises. This is the only way you can integrate this high cosmic energy. You are not alone in this process. All people will be confronted with this. Everyone will experience this process based on their current status of conscience. Confrontation with yourselves will make you closer to your sense of self. You will awaken from your own depth as a new, five-dimensional resident of Earth. In the scope of this, you can influence your environment. The resulting consequences for your society are obvious. Humans are at the focus of the new societies, and being human on Earth is taking the utmost propriety, always in harmony with Mother Earth. A global Earthly family can, and will, only develop from these pervasive processes of consciousness. Power and responsibility will pass to every individual, since every individual is a co-creator of the new octave of existence and a founder of their own new reality. Human civilisations will be transformed from the basis in order to create resilient communities that are able to handle this high energy.

You have completed plenty of work already. More still remains to be done. Be bold and confident. High energy will guide you and support you. It will wash you to the new shores of New Earth. This process started several decades ago. Now, it is rapidly picking up speed. Rooted well in the Here-and-Now, you will experience this quantum leap together with Earth. You will be able to enjoy it. The principle of enjoyment is of great importance. Awaken all your senses and discover your new path and your new existence.

Experiencing such a comprehensive evolutionary quantum leap is a blessing that is reserved for the Masters only. You are the star seed that has enabled this process of ascension. You are the founders of New Earth, the base generation that will enable a Golden Age on Earth. Future generations will look back with gratitude and honour you.

We Agarthans are deeply grateful to you. You enable us to contact Outer Earth again after this very long time of separation, in order to engage in a mutual loving exchange. Our future connection will be characterised by that incredible evolutionary pioneering spirit. We will turn our planet into the paradise of our home together with Mother Earth. In cooperation with our cosmic neighbours, our sector of the galaxy will blossom and radiate its Light far into the universe.

The evolutionary quantum leap that the human civilisations of Outer Earth are now performing is leaving the extra-terrestrial communities of Light deeply impressed. They bow down before you in respect. They are excited to soon consciously welcome the whole Earthly family into their midst.

You may find it quite disconcerting at first when your perception deviates from the three-dimensional pallet, when you are suddenly starting to perceive multi-dimensional interrelations. Your roots in Earth will stabilise you and allow you to enjoy this new way of seeing, and to participate in life in a more holistic manner. Some facts will be relativized, and your serenity will increase. Comprehensive knowledge of interrelations can only enrich you and enable you to deal with your lives more intensely. A great surge of consciousness is waiting just ahead. Some of you are already in the process of enjoying it, while others prefer to continue their blinkered lives, believing only what their reason permits. Everyone is subject to the accelerated energy, however. It will become more and more difficult to withstand this flow. The expanded multi-dimensional view will, of course, make it impossible to uphold certain paradigms you have been fed all your lives. Your view of things will be revolutionised, and some foundations of your beliefs will dissolve. It will surely take courage to deal with new approaches, and to put together a new world view. The three-dimensional world is slowly bidding you farewell, giving way to a multi-dimensional reality. This immense wealth belongs to you, as it does to all cosmic citizens. Make use of it, and immerse yourselves in this new reality. Enjoy it in full, and let the new paradigms teach you. With this scope, design your future existence on Earth. Open yourselves to these cosmic worlds, both in the micro and the macro areas. Become seers!

Agartha, a Supreme Land

I have told you a lot about your transformation. I have spoken about the transition of mankind of Outer Earth into a multi-dimensional existence. Your history is in the process of being re-written, which will make your understanding of your incredible current transformation clear. As I explained, the Agarthans have developed differently. We have withdrawn from the plunge into the depth of matter with its corresponding polarity, and continued our evolutionary path in the Fifth Dimension, with its multi-dimensional aspects. We Agarthans are also subject to polarity, but it is a harmonised polarity. This means that we know none of its excesses. This is why we are a peaceful and peace-loving people. We know no diseases or social injustice. Every Agarthan is fully responsible for themselves, their own people and for Earth. The spaces and tunnel systems we live in are multi-dimensionally aligned. They are compatible with cosmic wormholes. Three-dimensional eyes and scientific treatises on them cannot perceive them. Your current ascension into the Fifth Dimension will enable you to slowly grasp such multi-dimensional connections. The amplitude of your status of conscience will be essential to allow you a view of these multidimensional spaces. As your consciousness rises up, you will develop and integrate the cosmic love and cosmic compassion you need to develop an entirely different motivation in your exploration. Warrior-like reactions belong on Old Earth. The new era will be entirely free of them. Instead, there will be curious exploration of Earth and cosmic space in order to better get to know yourselves and your surroundings, and to feel embedded in a greater whole.

The close contact with cosmic and inner-terrestrial populations will strengthen your self-confidence in love. We are all connected to each other by the love of our creator. We act accordingly. This cosmic love will give the Earthly population a wonderful feeling of acceptance, comfort and fulfilment. You have spent a very long time separated from such a condition. The yearning for it is inherent in every individual. Now, it can finally be met.

We as Agarthans are entirely committed to Earth and to cosmic love. They are our providers and our fulfilment. The people of Outer Earth will also soon awaken to this awareness and adjust their lives accordingly. Of course, this will require some transformations and new structures, to get away from the current revolts and chaotic conditions. It will help you understand what is going on around the world right now. The societies of

Outer Earth adjust to New Earth. This must, by necessity, cause some changes. Stay calm, watch what is going on around you, and look at it from this perspective.

This pervasive, sustainable transformation is the basis needed to integrate and keep up with the accelerated high vibration. Your dues will be New Earth, along with access to cosmic multi-dimensionality. This will truly be a new beginning for all human societies and for Mother Earth herself. It will be a new beginning that will consciously open the gates to the cosmic societies of Light to you, resulting in your participation in the cosmic councils.

My dears, the time of separation has definitely come to an end. Your island existence is over! Yes, you have had to go through great changes, but you are now ready to experience great cosmic life tasks.

You will take gigantic steps to adjust to our level of consciousness. You are, and you have always been multi-dimensional beings that now remember their origins. We are all cosmic star seed that has developed here on and in Earth. Our joint development is the treasure of Earth that she will provide to the societies of Light. It will enrich the cosmos on its way to Light.

We of the population of the Agarthans, are very proud of our brothers and sisters of Outer Earth. We have great respect for your transformations and your drive to transfer Earth and her people into a level of existence within Light. We, too, are strongly involved in this process. We do our best to send five-dimensional energy through Earth in order to support you from inside of our planet as well. You are currently being supplied and energised from the cosmos as well as from Earth. Your bodies are being charged up with earthly and cosmic energy. These energies have a transformative effect. They will make your bodies compatible with the multi-dimensional requirements and re-align them to equip them with new tools. Those new tools include alignment and supplementation of your DNA, to aid your senses and guide them into the quantum levels to let you see. You will return to being what you once used to be. Your deep dive into matter has taught you plenty, and supplemented your cosmic potential. Now, you are once again ready to recover your true selves, and to continue to grow on the path of Light. Your journey into the dark has taught you the Light. Your yearning was your signpost and your companion. Welcome, dear brothers and sisters, in this new dimension of Light. Welcome home.

The population of Agartha is living in agrarian communities. We have no great conurbations. We are all connected to each other with our telepathic abilities. This is similar to your internet, but does not require the electronics you use. Every Agarthan is connected to this network and can engage in exchange with their people accordingly. We also have an economic system that helps people trade their goods and services among each other. While we also have a kind of currency, it is not comparable to the currencies of Outer Earth. It is merely a means trade that regulates needs among the Agarthans. When we speak of wealth, we mean our inner fulfilment and our love to creation. We barely have any material needs at all. Our evolutionary path has taught us to materialise our wishes and to subject them to the greater whole. We are not subject to any egotistical efforts. We act as a community – as a WE. You will also develop the evolutionary process from I to WE in the next few decades. This will make you compatible with the cosmic and innerterrestrial families. This focus will be entirely new for you, but it will reunify the human family. Our philosophy in life is still opposed to yours, but the path into Light, with all of your transformations that accompany it, will teach the civilisations of Outer Earth better ways.

You will recognise this pervasive transformation that you are currently undergoing. It will take some time. People are changing from the inside out through the cosmic vibrations. They will design their communities accordingly. All people will feel the need to adjust to the new laws of Light. It will liberate humans from their daily yokes, and they will recognise their inner fulfilment.

We Agarthans are a sensuous people. We love all kinds of art and expression. We go through life with great humour. We are released from existential pressures and can fully enjoy creation. Yes, we have preserved paradise for ourselves because we did not want to step into the cycle of matter. This paradise is what you are once more steering towards. You and your next generations will build their "Golden Age" on Earth and we, the Agarthans, will help you do so.

At the moment, you are building the foundations for your future paradise with your great transformations. The people of the Agarthans are connected to you on your path. We support you to the best of our abilities. Every individual can telepathically connect to us to ask us for advice or to simply engage with us in unconditional love. We are a great community in and on Earth. We travel through the cosmos with our motherly planet. The time has come to get to know each other better. We are a society united by our fate here on Earth. We explore the cosmos together and continue on our journey into Light.

Our love will connect to each of you. We are homesick for the people of Outer Earth. Soon, we will embrace each other once more. Your amnesia will be over!

I have good reason to call the habitat of the Agarthans a "Supreme Land". Isn't it wonderful to live in a paradisiacal community, liberated from existential and survival pressures and being able to focus on one's fulfilment? These qualities and modes of life are what we have developed and refined with the dimension available to us.

We, too, have developed further on our evolutionary path through the millennia, of course. We are in close contact with the cosmic families of Light, and we have developed the tools required for this, both spiritual and material, and mastered their use. We are also, however, in contact with the representatives of the spiritual hierarchy of Earth and the councils of our neighbouring planets. Cosmic cooperation is our desire. After all, are we not all connected in the ONE? Our multi-dimensional alignment enables us to travel into our solar system, as well as in territories farther away in our universe. Such journeys have taught us a lot. We have been able to integrate some impressions into ourselves and into our community. We are, as a result, a cosmically aligned community, just as you will become in future. Your access to multi-dimensionality will liberate you of your limitations and allow you to explore the numinous.

If you wish, we will gladly give you a hand in the beginning, supporting you as you try your legs. Our universe is not separate from Earth. It is ever-present here. Distances are obstacles or impairments only on the three- and four-dimensional levels. All is present in the Here-and-Now, influencing each other. An immense cosmic exchange between all planets and their residents is ever-present. This information now strongly influences the people of Outer Earth and helps them with this important transition into a higher octave of being. Soon, you will cast off the remaining veil of separation, to be able to consciously look your star family in the eye. They are here and there and everywhere. All is ONE. This is the multi-dimensional statement that will soon no longer be strange to you!

My dear people, even though you cannot enter our territory yet, we are still present with you on Outer Earth. It may still be difficult for us physically due to your current vibration. Spiritually, however, we are connected to you. We explore Outer Earth and get to know you and your communities. You are not strangers to us, but part of our Earthly family. We will gladly disclose ourselves to you, in order to allow you to re-embrace this once-lost part of your family. We are ONE with our Mother Earth. We are part of her.

The circumstances of your growth differ greatly from case to case. Some have been on their spiritual paths for a very long time. They have already passed through many personal transformations. Others still allow the high vibration to drive and harass them. Some individuals are abruptly growing up and will recognise the entire spectrum of their selves at once. No matter what your path in life entails: This high energy is entering your bodies and your self. Turning you into the multidimensional beings you were from the beginning.

The entire atomic structure of Earth is now being adjusted to the multi-dimensional level. Where necessary, it undergoes transformation. New learning experiences with yourselves, as well as with matter, are the consequences of this. Enjoy this new experience. It will show you the progressing vibrational amplitude. Quite a few slumberers will fluently awaken in the new reality of New Earth. Only by remembering their pasts will they become aware of the quantum leap they experience. Leaps of consciousness are liberating and exhilarating. They come with great feelings of pleasure, gratitude and love. The re-alignment of one's respective everyday lives is then a need, and a pleasure alike.

Your consciousness is progressing in great steps right now. This process is changing you as an individual, your personal lives, and the community in which you live. New structures of life will have to be found to live up to this consciousness. Never forget that you are not alone in this transformative process. All people of Outer Earth are part of this ascension. Earth in turn will go through its own five-dimensional adjustment, including its flora and fauna.

Earth will continue on her journey into Light wearing a new face and carrying a conscious mankind. She will travel the universe with us. Many new impressions will be integrated and expended by the cosmic game.

Diverse Intentions

This time characterised by innovation will now enable you to put innovative and unconventional ideas and projects into practice. The dissolution of old societal structures, the new way of handling matter, and your own liberation will give birth to entirely different models and projects in the long run. They will be able to better support reborn humans, and give greater joy in life. This joy in life is part of the liberating process you are going through. Seriousness and severity do not make for good incentives. The feeling of joy that your liberation will bring with it will motivate you to move what mountains remain that have no place in your new existence.

Listen to your inner voice and your intuition - follow its instructions. You will find that your fellow humans are undertaking similar efforts. The same evolutionary process binds you all together. There are no boundaries here! It will happen all around the world. The basic attitude will be globally consistent. It will happen similarly in every person, matching the tradition they practice. The basic attitude includes love for oneself, for mankind, and Earth, and the resulting responsibility. A responsible person can no longer be manipulated – neither socially, politically, nor religiously. Revolts, reformations and upheavals will shake up civilisations and help them develop a new, shared path. That new path will be taken by adult, responsible citizens who make sure that mankind and Earth remain well. A gigantic potential of talents and creative power will take hold of Earth and make it blossom. People will live and work together, joined in their love for Earth in spite of their different traditions. Destructive projects and scenarios that would be detrimental for Earth will be forestalled by her citizens. New, environmentally compatible technologies will enjoy priority in spite of tedious changes. Humans will shift from Earth's ruler to a scenario of cohabitation. They will recognise their symbiosis with Gaia and their responsibility for the next generations. This basic motivation will take hold of all people on Outer Earth. Love for Mother Earth is now being constantly ignited in every single heart.

The energy of your hearts will be the basis for the new era. This applies to all human matters and beyond. Even though intentions are diverse, they all have the same basic principle: The love for All-That-Is. The cosmic energy flowing onto Earth is an energy of the finest love. It will fulfil you and act through you. Unburden your physical heart from old ballast to let it absorb this wonderful energy and pass it on. This energy of the heart will transform and regenerate you, and your societies, in love. Compassion for your brothers and sisters will help you support even the weakest members of your communities, and to help them participate in the treasures of Earth. You are a wonderful Earthly community that is developing together and providing its treasures to Earth, as well as the innerterrestrial and the cosmic spaces.

The more you offer your treasures, providing them to contribute, the more generous this energy will flow in all directions. We are all only benefactors of divine creation, completing it to the best of our abilities.

Our contribution will support the next generations and enable them to supplement creation in their own manner. We are all divine co-creators under the direction of the cosmic energy of love. This energy of love is the building block of all of our creations, in material and spiritual respects alike. All is interwoven with everything else, and only the energy density differentiates it. It has always been this way. The humans of Outer Earth will only now become aware of it thanks to their higher vibration. Matter is condensed energy of love, as you can see. It knows no energetic separation. Over time, you will be able to change and model this matter in love. You will even be able to manifest it through the power of your thoughts. Only this unconditional love will enable you to creatively manifest your own ideas. The high cosmic vibrations of love that Earth is now absorbing is this unconditional love that Earth has not yet known. This cosmic quality of love can now pour down on the entire planet with the raised amplitude of Earth. It can nurture and fulfil her. A new facet of love is disclosed to mankind, breaking the boundaries of all that is known. You will surely find it easy to open yourself up to that love. Implementing it in your everyday lives will be the logical consequence. You are used to changes being accompanied by stress and suffering. Integration of the unconditional cosmic love, however, will fill your entire being. Calm and stability will follow. Like a dried-out sponge, you will be able to absorb this love once more. It is your divine return to your beginnings. It marks the end of a long separation. Cradled in cosmic love, you will implement the most diverse of intentions to the benefit of yourself and of Earth. Love will be your future motivation in all matters. The liberating gate is already open. Your hearts are yearning for those new cosmic vibrations of love. The societies of Outer Earth will awaken in the new era in love, and design them accordingly.

When your lives' plans are designed by the energy of the heart, they will be liberated from any egotistical efforts. They follow holistic and sustainable approaches. The energy of the heart is a connection between your reason and your emotions. In your heart, those qualities will be raised to a higher level and adjusted to the cosmic energy of love. They are, in a way, refined in this manner. Trust in this energy, even though it is still new to you. Open your hearts to your plans and your ideas. Listen and feel for the corresponding reactions. If your heart consents, you should proceed.

This, however, requires calm and rest. In fast-moving times like yours, rest and calm will become part of your mode of survival. They will give you the stability you need, and a higher perspective of events. Keeping an overview of what is happening will give you the serenity you need to actively implement your life plans, and to take action where your help is needed. A network of conscious Earthly citizens will be the pillar of your communities. The more consciously a community is living, the more serenely it can guide and control its own fate. The necessity of innovations of all kinds is understood and implemented by everyone. This way, it keeps from causing chaos and unrest. Every person is responsible for themselves and for their communities, but they need to develop that stability in their own selves first. Afterwards, they can share it with their surroundings. As I mentioned before, your personal work of consciousness is the basis for this new Earthly cycle. New Earth will take place inside every individual. It will not be consumed from the outside. This is the great quantum leap that every individual is going through right now.

Conscious human communities will understand the geophysical adjustments of Mother Earth. They will be able to protect themselves. After all, they will be in contact with themselves, their surroundings, and Earth. They will perceive the portents and warning signals, and draw conclusions from them. Consciousness means using all of one's senses and walking through life with an alert mind. It also means being open to new things. It means living in the Here-and-Now as well. This is the only moment that one can truly call life. The past and the future merge in the now. All is present in the moment. The more you grow into multi-dimensionality, the clearer this statement will become, and the more urgent its application will be. The current shift from a linear to a non-linear cycle is now present. It still causes confusion. Try seeing and understanding time increasingly as relative.

There is nothing more relative than time. Outer Earth is integrated into its own time mode, but we, the Agarthans, live near-timelessly in a continuum of generations. Our cosmic friends in turn have their own time matrixes to match their home planets. Every human being has their own time rhythm as well, though it is strongly influenced by the day/night conditions on Outer

Earth, as well as by societies' structures. You may have experienced the liberating feeling of slipping out of time, e.g. in long waking drams or unexpected events that had their own duration while only taking very few seconds in real time!

You will move increasingly into your own timelessness now, modelling and expanding it. You will do so in order to follow your dreams, to create projects and ideas with your thoughts, or to simply be embedded in a greater whole. Play with the relativity of time. Explore it. You are not victims of time. It is only a grid, a reference and a help in societal structures. Take your time and use it for your own good. Build those pleasurable islands in time where you can relax and break out of your often stressful everyday lives. Start experiencing the pleasant side of your lives. Make use of this immense treasure trove of joy and humour, and return to time, and your everyday lives, after regenerating.

The timeless and the temporal are present together in the Here-and-Now. The high energy will promote the timeless status. It is multi-dimensional. Multi-dimensionality has many facets that affect your everyday lives. Limitless exploration of their attributes will be fascinating for you. It will liberate you from your limiting world view. What a promising adventure you have started! Enjoy it to the fullest.

Effects on Earth and Her Inhabitants

The high cosmic vibration reaches every person, no matter where on Earth they live; but integration of this high, transforming vibration is, however, left to every individual. Humans are subject to the divine law of free will. Anyone who refuses to submit to their personal transformation and who prefers to remain in their old thought patterns will not be involved in this ascension into the higher octave of being. There will, therefore, be a span of time on Earth in which the Third and Fourth Dimensions will still be greatly present for many people, while others are already collecting experiences of the Fifth Dimension.

This discrepancy will be difficult or downright incomprehensible to New Earth and her reborn humans. There will be attacks on Gaia and her people, as they currently happen on Old Earth as well. You will find this transition period challenging. Remember that all people must open up to the new energy over time if they do not want to fall ill and have to leave the planet. Going against the flow will become extremely difficult with the strongly accelerated energy. Those people will be incompatible with the high energy, and such incompatibility will lead to restlessness and destructive effects, until those people are willing to adjust to the high energy. However, this will require them to let go of their claims to power. They will gain the understanding that all is interwoven. Their physical and social pressure will teach them to handle the new, high energy and to finally accept the new structures.

You are facing a restless time. I urge you to focus on your inner centre in order to weather these tensions well. Earth in turn is changing on a geophysical level to initiate her own rebirth, and to heal the wounds humans have given it. These shifts of Earth and the resulting floods will be a great challenge to the humans of Outer Earth. Try to protect your own stability and sensitivity. Use all your senses and perceive your environment and Earth properly. Recognise the portents of change. The better you integrate the high vibration inside you, the better will you be able to use your new tools. I am thinking in particular of your expanded DNA with its multi-dimensional benefits, and the expanded sensibility and sensitivity that follows.

The discrepancy of the different vibrational amplitudes is great. For the last eons, humans have remained on a very heavy and polarised energy density. Their current ascension to the Fifth Dimension offers mankind a previously unknown high and light energy density that is truly impossible to compare to the old one. This causes great transformation work in every single person. They will have to go through this on their own. Of course, integration of these high Light particles will help them adjust their bodies and minds to the new energetic conditions. In the end, however, everyone will have to make their own decision as to whether they want to take this important evolutionary step or not.

Many feel that it would be easier to remain in their familiar prisons than to venture out to conquer unknown, liberating territories. Yes, it does take courage and confidence to get to know oneself anew and to let those new findings influence one's environment. It will lead to personal and social changes on a great scale. Superficially, this will lead to unrest and chaos. A new global and sustainable society can only be achieved by great changes. In the long term, the human civilisations on Outer Earth will, however, be liberated politically, religiously and socially. An Earthly population that can unfold freely, and that knows neither hunger nor war, is a goal worth any effort to achieve.

The continuous shower of high cosmic energy will make it hard for any individual to remain buried in their old world view. They will have to fight the change.

Instead of experiencing victory, they will only waste energy needlessly. Therefore, try to consciously flow with this high energy. Be grateful that it shows you where you need to transform. Like a caterpillar morphs into a butterfly, you will find in surprise after a few years that you have quickly developed into a cosmic global citizen. You will be free from burdens from Old Earth and free to conquer and integrate the new multi-dimensional level. Evolution cannot be prevented. It can only be delayed. Cosmic effects are currently at work on Earth. They will blast away the borders of the three-dimensional human thought patterns.

Only on the level of the soul can you feel that you are living here on Earth in the right moment to make your contributions to the whole. This inner-most trust in you will give you the courage and confidence to travel this very personal path during this time of ascension, while also enjoying it. You will now truly experience the most intense and interesting time that Earth has ever seen. Be aware of this. Experience it with every fibre of your bodies and your senses. Connect to this loving cosmic energy and transform into the universal cosmic beings you once were and that you will soon return to being. This will be a conscious return to the cosmic fold of your star families, and a true coming home.

Your inherent yearning for unification with All-That-Is will increasingly often be the driving force that urges you to connect to Earth and to the cosmos. Call it your divine yearning or your claim to merge with the ONE. The ONE is everywhere, contained in every single one of you. The ONE is the energy of love that connects all atoms throughout the cosmos. Our creator is not found outside of us. We are part of them. Progress of consciousness that we are currently subject to will overcome the three- and four-dimensional patterns of separation, show you and let you feel that you are co-creators here on Earth, and that you consciously contribute to designing the divine plan of creation. What a wonderful responsibility you are taking over now, to give our Mother Earth the respect she is due, and to give human civilisations a fulfilling and liberating lifestyle. May the high Light particles be integrated as fully as possible by everyone, to soon allow mankind to design their future freely. This way, the path to the "Golden Age" of Earth can be prepared and initiated for the coming generations.

An adult mankind will no longer be able to stand any manipulative power structures. Every individual will have come into their own power, and their own responsibility. Do not underestimate humans! Every single person has a gigantic potential of talents that they have acquired through all terrestrial and cosmic incarnations. These treasures will once again be available to them, thanks to the accelerated energy. The separation from your various life cycles is over. All is present in the Here-and-Now. Consciously approach your preferences, recognise your inherent talents, and reactivate them by training. Every person is a universe in themselves, connecting with the greater universe. All is connected and interlinked. All is present and available in the Here-and-Now. This understanding is just beginning to awaken in humans. It will release great potentials that will benefit global mankind and Earth. All that you do for yourself, for your society and for Earth is also done for your stellar families and the residents of Inner Earth. Your growth processes and awakening into the greater whole will give cosmic space an incredible burst of Light. We are all part of each other. We look forward to continuing on our shared path into Light, strengthened by our brother and sisters of Outer Earth. Mutual support is the most natural thing in the cosmos. This will soon be handled the same way on Outer Earth. After all, you are going on a journey into Light together with Gaia.

Unyielding positions of power will put their strain on humans. However, they will find ways to maintain their inner peace. They will work their way towards liberation into an existence worthy of humans in small steps. Global linking between people will contribute as well, to initiate gradual development of democratic structures around the world. The energetic connection between humans will make this process happen relatively quickly, supported by high cosmic vibrations that are now flushed onto Earth. Stay confident and support your global co-residents on Earth to let them feel your compassion and this family-like network.

This time of transformation will bring the people of Outer Earth close together. All of mankind will come to see themselves as an Early Family, and will offer support to their citizens who are weaker than them. This is a highly valuable process towards becoming a cosmic citizen of Earth who will soon merge with their families of Light.

You must experience this brother- and sisterhood on Earth before you can all connect to the cosmic and innerterrestrial space together. This is, in a way, a prerequisite. It will teach you plenty of tolerance and acceptance for your diverging life forms. Humanity as such will move to the centre in future. Ethnicity or association with cultures and traditions will become irrelevant. This is a five-dimensional quality that will become established and prevail on Earth.

This sustainable process that is now running through all your communities and civilisations is targeted at the global Earthly family with all the different structures and traditions. This is a great wealth that all humans will benefit from. It will strengthen them in their self-perception as citizens of Earth.

In spite of the current chaos and revolts, this time of transformation will eventually bring the desired global peace to the humans of Outer Earth, and support them in their humanity.

Alterations

As soon as you have integrated a greater share of cosmic Light particles into your bodies and your minds, you will change into new, five-dimensional humans. You will go through physical and mental changes. You will feel lighter and more transparent. Your physical energy density will be refined. This means that you will perceive your surroundings increasingly through your physical structure as well. Your restrictions will soften, and you will increasingly connect to All-That-Is. This connection to the whole will also affect your minds. This will enable you to connect emotionally not only to your surroundings, but also on a global level. You will perceive the worries and needs of residents of Earth who are far away. You will be able to help them emotionally, but also in a material respect. We on Earth are one interconnected human society. Like we, the Agarthans, are closely connected to you and know your worries and needs, you will know those of your fellow humans. The cosmic Light particles to be integrated are made up of cosmic love and cosmic compassion. You will not suffer with your fellow humans, but support them in love and compassion on their evolutionary path. This support also means that every person can choose their own path freely. Everyone has the right to their own learning processes. A loving hand will always be welcome in difficult learning processes, though the person affected will have to walk their path on their own. Being certain that we are ONE family on Earth will strengthen the population of our dear planet. Together, we are bold and self-confident. These qualities will give you the strength to better understand yourselves and to create innovative structures for your new societies. An internally interwoven Earthly community needs new guidelines that surpass all borders for its reference. The feeling of unity will take hold of mankind, no matter their different traditions and ethnicities. All humans will be at the focus, whether they are women, men, or children of any age group.

Everyone is looking back at a long, cosmic biography with innumerable learning processes in all sorts of situations. These learning processes refine every incarnated soul until it definitively merges back into our source, the ONE. We all contribute to enriching our source, and praising our divine refuge. This is how you will recognise your co-residents. This is what will make you treat them with respect and love. As soon as the veil of three- and four-dimensional separation has been lifted from you, you will understand this connection and act accordingly. This is the general innovation that will give you a peaceful span here on Earth that will last many generations. It will be your great reward after the strenuous time of ascension into a new level of existence.

Innovations in all areas of your everyday lives will let you soar. Handling of matter will become much simpler for you due to its spiritualisation. Things will change in your relationships as well. Harmonisation of polarities and liberation of restriction structures, as well as obsolete traditions, will see to this. Harmonisation of female and male polarity will reduce tension among the genders. Trust in mutual love and respect will increase. New families will thrive again and provide a nest of calm and stability to their children. Humans will be at the centre of attention, no matter their gender, age or income. Everyone will find their income where they feel well cared for and able to follow a fulfilling career. Social structures will be characterised by responsibility and help people reacquire their independence. Harmonisation of polarities will, of course, also fundamentally change your economic, political and religious lives. Excesses will be firmly in the past.

These structures will be adjusted to the needs of the general good. This will ensure a constructive and peaceful cohabitation. With every individual taking responsibly, laws will be rendered unnecessary and obsolete.

Your focus will be the individual, and peaceful cohabitation of all the different civilisations on Earth. Each community will contribute its talents and fruits to the greater whole. A great wealth of exchange will nurture and educate all people. It will enable them to liberate themselves from their existential pressures. That pressure prevents spiritual further development of an individual, leaving them caught in matter. Dealing with the arts, the humanities and nature is sustenance humans need just as much, in order to lead further developed and fulfilling lives.

As you can see, the innovations will affect all areas of your personal lives, as well as that of the entire Earthly community. Learning new things, acquiring new technologies and models for interaction will be your companions in the near future. Many new achievements in all areas will be created by people in order to permit a better global cohabitation here on Earth. A broad range of innovative and sustainable products will be made available to mankind. The joy in learning and playing will be ever-present again. Life on Earth is like a passionate game. It means exploring this existence and the superordinate spheres. It means submerging oneself in matter, but also going on explorative flights into etheric and higher-dimensional worlds. Mother Earth is our "home port". She serves as the starting point and the destination for our adventures.

Changes on a greater scale must be expected from Earth as well. She has already spent several years adjusting to the five-dimensional level. This includes topographical changes and her axial alignment. Climate changes have resulted from this. The affected populations will find them to be severe challenges at times. They may even force populations to leave their homes. The Earth's population will have to deal with these great migrations and provide a new home to such humans. We are all pulling on the same string here. This is the only way we can survive. Mankind will have to move closer in order to grant every individual their right to live here on Earth.

This will cause your hearts to open and inspire compassion for the worries of your neighbours. The higher dimensions will be lived from the level of the heart. This will be new to the humans of Old Earth. The level of the heart will be the platform of your future activities and relationships. The cosmic quality of unconditional love will now slowly become anchored on Earth and guide you in your interaction with yourself and your environment. In spite of the great changes ahead, you will not handle them with your old and limiting emotions, but initiate new services of cosmic love. The hearts of all residents of Terra will merge and the resources of Earth will be shared among them all. This new earthly community will take care of the planet Earth and deal with cosmic space responsibly as well.

You will intuitively recognise the growth and adjustment processes of Earth and support them on her order. You will start consciously living the symbiosis with Earth. You will recognise the changes in advance, based on the warning signals sent to you. You are spirit in matter. You will start out by exploring your share in Earth, your bodies, in order to then become familiar with the surrounding matter as well. Matter is nothing but condensed energy of love that now spiritualised and can be replaced and modelled with your spirits. Your spirit and matter are not separate from each other. Everything is interwoven. The divine is ever-present. It is reflected in every single atom. You are divine co-creators and the architects of New Earth. Take divine responsibility and create your new home planet – your new home – together with Mother Earth. Respect Mother Earth as a divine being that is going on her evolutionary path into Light, just as you are.

The clear feature of the new level of existence is the removal of your feeling of being separate from All-That-Is. The low vibrational density did not allow you to have a look into integrated perspectives. You were virtually locked into a narrow system with borders and rules. The cosmic energy now flushed onto Earth has the potential to break open borders. The humans of Outer Earth are transferring to the status of adults, with all the responsibility that goes with it. You will find this liberation in yourselves at first, before it will affect your environment and your societies. Every individual has a lot of transformation work in store for them. Your communities will have to restructure as well, however, to give every human their right to responsibility and conscious life. Humans will no longer accept suppression of these rights. They will successfully fight any such efforts. The time of gurus and potentates in any area is finally coming to a close.

As your DNA breaks up, you will revert to the multi-dimensional cosmic beings that feel their connection to All-That-Is, willing to develop their life goals responsibly together with the whole. Your cosmic potential will be available to you once again. It will pervasively change human civilisations and offer a reborn community of Earth a way to integrate the cosmic matrix of Light on Earth.

The paradise code that is resting in every individual is now slowly waking from its long hibernation. It will let humans and Earth blossom. Spring has come. A new world cycle is ahead. It will guide our sun with our planetary system into the worlds of Light. Cosmic influences will challenge Mother Earth and her humans. They will also give them this opportunity of setting out on a great evolutionary journey. Gratitude for being allowed to experience and help design this incredible transition will take hold of conscious humans, motivating them to go on their journeys in light of this.

Embedded into the cosmic family of Light, the citizens of Earth will consciously experience their cosmic love and compassion. It's a wonderful feeling of belonging and being kept safe that will nurture and invigorate humans. A long-existing yearning has finally been quenched.

No Compromises

The high cosmic vibration that is now flooding Earth and penetrating into each and every atom not only changes human individuals, but also their societies and the planet as a whole. Fighting this strong vibration is useless and devoid of any sense of reality. You now need to learn to live with the new reality of change. You must make the best of it for yourselves and for your environment. This evolutionary push knows no compromises. It has a superordinate, cosmic goal that involves all families in space and all planets. The changes and challenges that are now happening on Earth are a gift and a blessing for the human civilisations of Earth. It will finally allow you to experience five- and even higher-dimensional levels, and to leave your status as toddlers. Once you look at this important evolutionary step from a higher perspective, you will find your challenges relativized. You will be grateful for being allowed to experience and contribute to the design of this historic time with Earth. It is all a matter of perspective that will allow you to leave the role of victim, and step into that of a cosmic co-creator.

The better an individual integrates this high vibration into themselves, the more stably will they ride this cosmic wave, and be able to enjoy it. Integration of this vibration takes time and effort, and an interest in one's own internal matters in order to get rid of old ballast such as outdated behavioural patterns and fears. You will then be able to take up this high vibration once more. Your vessel will only be able to absorb new things if you let go of the old and obsolete.

The high vibration may change your bodies and minds, but every individual must get rid of their accumulated burdens. You are now shifting into the status of conscious adults with all the responsibility this entails. You cannot somehow cheat to get to this new level. You must take your path consciously and without compromises. This will lead to great societal and religious changes that will initiate the new five-dimensional Earth.

This high vibration is taking hold of the entire planet. It will bring about global changes. Change is expected in all matters where human communities live on Earth.

Our dear planet, whether you call her Earth, Terra, or Gaia, is changing into the status of a star. We will all be allowed to accompany her and to participate in her cosmic journey. Awaken, dear residents of Outer Earth! Awaken from your long magical sleep, and recognise the signs of the time. Understand the rebirth of Earth into a higher octave of being. The times of repression, playing down, or ignoring are over. The door to a new space has opened and is beckoning!

Not making compromises means that every person will have to deal with themselves and their lives here on Earth. They must develop clarity in their ideas and wishes, in order to bring about the changes needed. This is about how to design one's life. It will cause limitations and obstacles to withdraw from you. The positive approach will guide energy into the future projects and withhold energy from abuse.

The high vibrational amplitude of Earth will make your ideas and thoughts faster to implement. They will manifest exponentially when a group of people has similar ideas and ideals. Reformation and revolution will now happen speedily. The same is true of implementation of new, sustainable concepts. The responsibility for these innovations is with the humans who create them. Every community will change sustainably from the inside out in this way, and take responsibility for this as well.

Responsibility for your thoughts is central as well. Focus your ideals for yourselves and your community. Remember the good of Earth. Concepts and innovations that are sustainable and serve the good of humans and

Earth will survive this time of transition and form the basis of future vibrational adjustments. Execution of egotistical concepts will become difficult. They will end up being impossible to implement, the high five-dimensional vibration will only permit projects that serve the greater good. Humans will learn to work towards the good of the whole, which includes the good of the individual. Borders between countries and continents will blur. The global good of humans and Earth will be at the focus. You are all connected and linked. You are responsible for the whole together. This is why the good of Earth must take priority throughout the planet. Neglect will affect all humans. The consciousness of the global citizen of Earth will now exponentially become part of all communities. In spite of different traditions and ethnicities, they will acquire a self-understanding as a citizen of Earth, with different approaches to problems. Listen to the indigenous peoples of Earth. They have preserved their access to Mother Earth. They can help you recover the direction you have lost, to return to her and support her on her evolutionary path.

You are now experiencing rebirth of yourselves. Old, obsolete patterns and models of thought cannot survive. A new human will move into the five-dimensional level, liberated from limiting thought patterns and attitudes towards life. You will first be released from your old selves This will, by necessity, influence your communities. Your new communities will therefore be renewed from the inside out. This is the prerequisite for a truly democratic cohabitation on Earth. The old democracies will also be required to adjust to the high vibration. The party systems will lose in power. Coexistence between people will take priority. Specialists of their respective subjects will take care of the matters of a community, and provide their knowledge to the whole. Superordinate perspectives such as the good of Earth as a whole, the cosmic space, but also the ethereal levels, will become part of your intents and projects. More and more, scientific findings will be involved in order to analyse the feasibility and sustainability of projects. Such scientific findings will soon make incredible progress. They will be facing multi-dimensional conditions that the science of Old Earth could barely guess at.

Fundamentally new conditions must be analysed. The new level must be felt and tried out before projects are assessed for feasibility. A comprehensive range of your abilities and talents will be involved in this feasibility, enabling you to create entirely new projects. Your intuition will be involved just as much as your reason and your feelings. The new models will be tracked in an integrated manner in order to achieve the greatest benefit for Earth and for mankind. Many new and interesting learning experiences are ahead of you to let you study the new spiritualised matter and to achieve the best possible results with it.

Some old insights will be put aside without compromise. They will be limited to a strongly historical value. They will belong to a different era of Earth. Each epoch creates its own tools and its own art. The new Earthly cycle will have a greater pallet of sounds and colours and an unlimited perspective and spiritualised matter. It will be an incredible treasure trove for scientists and artists, but also for every other person.

This refusal of compromise is a blessing for human civilisations. It is a break of old conditions that will allow the birth of innovative and new paradigms of life. The harmonisation of polarities caused by vibrations will make men and women into architects of the new Earthly cycles. All over Earth, women will spread their responsibility across their communities and countries. The feminine and masculine aspects will develop a basis of community that will work for all humans in harmony. Patriarchal societies of Old Earth will, of course, be subject to greater changes. They, too, will find that the high vibration will affect them without compromise. Their rebirth will also happen quickly. Because of this, the current generation of women must take caution and will need mutual support from men. Men and women will wonderfully supplement each other in their efforts for a new society. They will work for their own good and for the good of the whole at the same time. Tensions and suppression are no longer part of the new vibrational density. The corresponding traditions and rituals will dissolve.

No human will retain power over any other humans, no matter if they are men, women, or children. All humans are divine incarnations on Earth. They represent this divinity in their societies. Every human being is a divine co-creator in their lives and their environments. They will be respected as such. Human coexistence will undergo fundamental changes due to this. Everyone will freely choose the destiny of their own life. This is how they will contribute to their living communities. This freedom is your birth right as divine co-creators, and the basis for functional communities. Living with responsibility for oneself, one's community, and Earth is freedom. Such responsible humans will be the pillars of your future societies and civilisations on which New Earth will rest.

Even though the current transformations are challenging for you, keep an eye on this future perspective, and develop the changes in the midst of your families. Support each other and find your shared, parallel path into your personal Freedom. Freedom is a high asset that is lived respectfully and responsibly with the whole. A free Earthly community will be able to live its potential in full. It will be able to provide it to humans and to Earth with generosity. An incredible wealth of resources can be implemented creatively.

Love will be the bond of your connections and obligations to accept yourself. Love will be the basis of new communities and your primary energetic sustenance. Without love, Earth and her humans would still be caught in the darkest of ages. Love is your future and your reason for existence here on Terra. Love will permit our shared unification and merger with the cosmic civilisations. We are all connected in love in the ONE. In love, we will all continue on our path into Light, to our source, our creator god/creator goddess, the great AHAU.

Our shared, connecting love will open the gates to Agartha and finally bring a loving Earthly family back tougher. We yearn to embrace you. The hope to see you again soon motivates us. Our love for the humans of Outer Earth permeates our planet, flowing into your hearts. Listen to our heartbeats. Listen to the vibration of love that is now rising in you. We are here!

Supplies

The energy currently being flushed onto Earth will replenish all imaginable resources that our planet, and her residents, need to enjoy five- and multi-dimensional levels. Among other things, this is the higher Light quality that is made up of cosmic information as well as the quality that your eyes can perceive. Your eyes will perceive a greater range of life on Earth, in the form of colours, as well as in spherical form. This means that you will increasingly meet ethereal beings that belong to Earth now, as well as energy patterns. You will become aware of the energetic emanations of Terra and, in part, be able to recognise them by looking at them. Matter will cease to be dead material to you, but become an invigorated partner. Your senses will continually refine and let you recognise your surroundings, as well as yourselves, more deeply. The better you can integrate the high cosmic energy into yourselves, the more quickly you will grow into this new level of existence, and the better you will be able to recognise and comprehend yourself and Earth in a more faceted manner. You are about to start gradually looking through the veil of separation, and to spy realities that are new to you.

A great new reality will become evident to you and show you that life on Earth has more layers than you have ever been able to suspect. This will expand the horizon of your knowledge and enable you to tackle holistic scientific studies in order to better understand nature and matter. Humans will also find the inexplicable suddenly become real. It may not be tangible, but it can be seen and felt. This includes geometrical energy patterns, auras, and creatures from other dimensions of life. Our Earth hosts many residents from different dimensional levels and timelines. All is present in the Here-and-Now, and has always been. Now, you will finally become aware of it. This process will take place step by step as energy increases. You will get the time you need to adjust. The energetic connection to All-That-Is is a fact that you will now become aware of unambiguously.

A new clarity of personal living conditions will therefore help you better design your lives and harmonise them with the whole. Birth, death, and resurrection are the natural paradigms of physical living conditions on Earth. The ethereal living conditions are subject to different paradigms, but all terrestrial living conditions are based on unconditional love as a basic sustenance and existential matrix.

As I have mentioned several times so far, divine love permeates all of your matter. Your being is based on this love, just like everything that surrounds you. In the third and fourth dimensions, this fact was difficult to comprehend for you. You were exposed to great pain and suffering due to the great polarity. The energy of New Earth will, however, reconcile you to your memories. Entirely new experiences are awaiting you. They will reveal this love to you and fill your hearts. This unconditional cosmic love, coupled with cosmic compassion, will be radiated by your hearts. It will connect the populations of Outer Earth and nurture them. The quality of your hearts will permeate all of your relationships and projects. It will create your desired Garden of Eden on Earth. This Earthly community created by you will make its contribution that will connect all populations of Inner and Outer Earth, as well as the cosmic families.

The connection to all populations of Light therefore happens from the inside out. It will not be forced on you from the outside. This great and conscious process of love will open the gates to your families of Light.

The ethereal beings that populate Earth are also divine creations of love. They support Earth and her residents on their path. Your conscious mutual cooperation will help you nurture and protect your communities. They will disclose their treasures to you and help build New Earth. The qualities of their existence are love and compassion.

The spectrum of life that has now been expended for you holds many new and loving things in store for you. The procedures of the old era will be transformed to give way to new approaches. Follow the path of love in your lives, and recognise this new facet of unconditionality in love that is now absorbing Earth.

Open your hearts and dance into the new octave of being. Enjoy the feeling of being protected, and of belonging to this wonderful, integrated population of earth, and to All-That-Is. Let your own inner sun shine and merge with the people and the cosmic suns. The solar aspect of humans will now step into the foreground, melting away all that is negative, in order to make space for a new co-existence.

Energy patterns of Earth, such as eddies, sheet-like emanations, and direct flows, are presently spread across the planet. Your ancestors knew them and built their places of ritual on them. They recognised the strength of Mother Earth and knew that they could use such forces for their own good. They also understood that human evolution was connected to Earth, and that they were moving along their cosmic path with her.

This original knowledge was unfortunately lost in many places, as modern mankind fixated on matter. The indigenous peoples of Earth have preserved this treasure of knowledge in many places. They will be of great help for you on your future paths. They know about the properties and effects of manipulation that is not wholesome for Mother Earth. They also know how to support her, protect her, and nurture her. They have been living in symbiosis with her for millennia. They are part of her, and they love her just as we, the Agarthans, do. You need to go beyond a rational procedure in order to get to know Mother Earth better. Most of all, you need love.

You will also need all your senses. The indigenous peoples of Earth are now ready to share their incredible treasure of knowledge with you. Mother Earth is, after all, the home planet for all of us. She is our provider and part of our selves. The devastating separation of a great part of the Earthly population from Mother Earth has caused pervasive damage to her. Now, the time has come to deliberately remind you of your roots and to apply the corrections needed to make sure that humanity once again pays her the respect and valuation that she is due.

Changes to your consumption behaviours and unconscious waste of your resources will keep you very busy in the near future. You will learn to live with Earth, rather than against her, even if this will have consequences for your everyday lives. The well-being of Earth will take priority. If Earth is well, then her people will be well, too. This principle will reach all minds and spark sustainable development.

Places of power that are spread across Earth are places to remember your roots and your Earthly selves. Contact Mother Earth and let her energy flood you. Absorbing her energy is remedial. It will give you the strength you need to continue to the evolutionary cosmic path and to enjoy it. Gaia is the closest representative of unconditional cosmic love. She is part of you, and you are part of her. This holistic acceptance will ignite your love for Gaia and keep you warm. Gaia is one of the most beautiful planets in our solar system. She is your home.

Even though the current changes and transformations are challenging for you: Continue on your journey to learn about yourself with confidence. What a gift it is to be involved in this historical turning point of Earth and to be able to help design it. Your soul will emerge from this transformation process much enriched, and provide this wealth to our source. No matter where on Earth you are living, you will develop your own personal process of growth and let it flow into your surroundings. Your divine selves with all of their experiences from all incarnations will merge with your higher-vibrational body. Your body is now ready to absorb its divinity! This is another separation that is now over. Unimaginable innovations can now be created from inside you. Divine co-creatorship of all humans will lead Earth and her populations into the "Golden Age", to let the terrestrial civilisations and Gaia blossom.

The five-dimensional level is the gate to multi-dimensionality and unlimited cosmic space with all its civilisations. Micro- and macrocosm will now be available to you for extensive scientific and ethereal journeys. The gates of the multiverse will now be open to you, with or without your bodies. Your spirituality will make quantum leaps. The higher levels are love itself, which you will get to know deeply now and integrate it in your lives. The terrestrial effects of your experience with love will connect Earth and humans ever more closely to our creator. The gold of love in your hearts will permeate our planet and make all of earth shine brightly. Our home planet will shine deeply into our universe and embrace our cosmic neighbours in love. Future cosmic exchange with our star families will be characterised by love.

This love will provide you with new stellar technologies and teach humans how to use them on Terra as well. These highly qualified technologies can only be used in love. They require a corresponding amplitude of love between the respective humans and their planet. Love on Terra is your future. This is true in all areas of human living conditions.

This amplitude of love from the humans of Outer Earth will also make it possible to finally open the sealed gates to the population of Agartha, permitting the unification of all residents of Terra.

Effects of Interstellar Communication

Our dear Earth is embedded in a greater structure of bodies that you call our solar system, our galaxy and our universe. These designations are perfectly correct. The interaction between all of those bodies, however, is still rather unclear to the humans of Outer Earth. Only the effects of our sun have been subject to research for a long time. Our solar system is a group of planets located at the outer fringe of our galaxy. The energy level of this zone matches this location. This means that a planet can be in a three- and four-dimensional vibrational density.

The current increase of the vibrational density will cause Terra to leave this energy density, and to develop further on higher levels of existence. She receives this energy surge from the galactic centre and the orbit of Earth around our central sun that places her closer at the centre. The closer a planet is to the centre, the more spiritual its vibrational density will be. Our entire solar system is in the process of taking this evolutionary leap. The corresponding adjustments must be performed throughout the planet. Matter will be more strictly spiritualised by this and will be subject to changed paradigms.

This spiritualisation of matter will permeate a planet. Its effects are not limited to the surface. We Agarthans and other residents of our solar systems that live inside their planets will, therefore, experience these changes and learn to handle them. The more spiritualised a population is, however, the better they will be able to adjust to this change. The people of Outer Earth, however, will find this adjustment to be a quantum leap and a rebirth into a new era of being. They will have to re-learn everyday activities, and feel their way around matter to design it to their wishes.

As our solar system ascends, our sun is keeping control. It keeps us informed with its rays and its energetic emanation. It in turn is nurtured and informed by our central sun, the galactic suns and the galactic centre. There is enormous interaction in terms of stellar communication that connects the celestial bodies to each other. It guides them on their evolutionary paths. This includes all kinds of radiation and forces of attraction. It also includes the corresponding resonance of the respective bodies. It is a give and take of our creator, and a manifestation of their love. Nothing happens by chance. All things are subject to divine orchestration and will fit into the universal matrix of love. From a human point of view, these cycles are invisible. They go beyond the capacity of linear thought that is inherent in three- and four-dimensional energy density.

Cosmic cycles such as the orbit of our Earth around our central sun are extremely long for humans in a linear time structure. Only a small fraction of that span can be historically tracked, since one pass around our central sun takes more than 26,000 years.

This so-called world year sees diverse civilisations come, each with their own evolutionary status. Earth is entering into a new world year with the Age of Aquarius. She is therefore moving more closely to our central sun. The radiation of our central sun is now stronger, enabling us to absorb cosmic energy and information unhindered. This leads to the current adjustments and transformations of Mother Earth and her residents. All populations of Earth are now getting to enjoy this high vibrational cosmic energy of love. We are all adjusting to this high vibration. Terra must also adjust to this increased vibration. Earth and climate changes follow suit. The increasingly frequent weather anomalies, volcanic eruptions, and earthquakes must be viewed in this context. This is part of our home planet adjusting to the new energetic paradigms.

The residents of Earth are, therefore, also subject to great adjustments. This high information of love that we now receive from the cosmos will change every individual and all civilisations alike. The future of us all will be love in all of its facets. This high vibration will also permit us to directly interact with the cosmos. All old limitations and separations are going to dissolve. We will all once again become a conscious part of the whole. We will find our places and contribute accordingly.

This perspective is to show you that cosmic projects cannot be forestalled. Our Earth is ascending into the Fifth Dimension, with the view of all the higher dimensions in our universe. Every human has the choice of joining her on this path, or of choosing a different planet with three- and four-dimensional learning processes. Every incarnated soul has their own personal learning mission and personal learning target. They are, therefore, choosing their own consequences. Your soul-selves will increasingly connect to your bodies due to the high vibrations. You will increasingly feel your divinity, and act accordingly. The veil of separation will dissolve and offer you the entire view of your incarnations, no matter if they come from Earth or from the cosmos. Your memory awakens and will show you a new feeling of the interconnections of your current lives and your past. It is a past that is present in the Here-and-Now, but not in a linear manner of thinking.

Linear thought will now be replaced by a multi-dimensional view. Awakening in these quantum magnitudes will make many things appear relative. It will grant you a holistic view of the whole. This connection to All-That-Is and the interaction of all dimensions in the Here-and-Now are building blocks for your future projects. Your intellect, as well as your emotions, will be revolutionised by an entirely new view of things. Recognising and feeling one's own identity as a multidimensional being will surpass your personal limitations and open up access to new worlds for you. No matter where those worlds are, they are also present in the Here-and-Now. They will become your contacts without surpassing any distances. The micro- and macrocosm are open to you. Explore yourselves, and All-That-Is with this unconditional love. Receive the cosmic vibrations of love that permeate and surround you. See with your hearts to let restrictions melt away and open up access to territories that are still unknown to you.

We Agarthans, for example, are such territories. So are your stellar families of Light, no matter where in the cosmos they are located. The eternity of the cosmos will be defined and thereby made possible for you to experience. This is a difficult statement for linear thought. I am aware of it. Let the multidimensionality, which is still unknown to you, surprise you. First, enjoy your regained freedom to the fullest. You will surely understand that this new way of thinking and feeling no longer permits any economic, social or religious suppression.

Stellar communication will be sent to every living being and into all matter by our sun. Cosmic information will reach even the darkest corner, transforming all with its quality of love. Love will bring us back together after separation. We will once again unite with our cosmic families of Light. The call of our creator god/creator goddess will guide and lead us on our further journey into Light. We will do our best to walk this holy path as co-creators.

Love is the essence of this process of ascension that you and Earth are now going through. Meet the changes required of you now in love, and trust in your own path and the path of mankind. The more lovingly you continue on your journey, the more harmonious the transformation processes you are about to experience will be. Love, acceptance and respect for yourself are the conditions to change your community and mankind as a whole. We are all connected to, and interwoven with, each other. This is why we all feel the loving transformations of every individual. This is the responsibly borne by every single human being. This is where stepping into the status of adult humans begins.

The Last Piece of the Puzzle

If you look at the evolutionary history of our Earth from a higher perspective, you will see that it is just facing the decisive phase in a quantum status. This means that her matter will now irrevocably be changed and transformed into a vibrational density of higher vibrations. This process commenced eons ago. It started out very slowly, but caused continual acceleration of the energy. This acceleration of energy has now reached the desired frequency in order to successfully tackle the last great transformations and adjustments. The face of Earth, as well as her inside, will now be adjusted to the necessary frequency. This permits our planet to participate as a partner in the cosmic change of planets and to reposition herself on her journey into Light. Of course, this is done in the group of her solar system, with which she is closely connected. This family cohesion provides stability within the cosmic rotations of planets, enabling the continuation of this journey of unconditional love.

Terra is a divine creature of her kind, following her divine fate in the dance with other planets of her solar system. She will align herself with the galactic centre once more and enjoy its emanations without restriction. She will, in a way, be taken by the hand into by the motherly bosom of our galaxy, in order to reach the path on which she is to continue into higher spheres. The last piece of the puzzle is your current extreme acceleration of energy that will give her the push she needs to enter the higher-vibrational regions of the galaxy. The more spiritualised a planet is, the greater the requirements to any residents she may have. The residents of Earth approved of these requirements on the level of their souls. Every soul incarnated on Earth is aware of the current fate of Earth and has agreed to consciously or unconsciously contribute to it in some form.

We – all residents of Earth – adjust to this high energy and try to progress on this journey into Light with it. We provide mutual support, both among each other and with Mother Earth. Some foolish, unconscious procedures in personal or global manners that would harm Earth and her people will no longer be tolerated. They will have no basis for realisation. A consensus of peace and respect towards every individual will spread across the planet like wildfire, destroying and dissolving claims to power. Our journey into Light will have direct consequences on your personal everyday lives and on the global situation.

Earth is now undergoing severe changes, as are her civilisations. We are all aligning ourselves with our galactic centre, our motherly bosom. We will only be able to continue our evolution with Mother Earth. This is a great, cosmic gift. Our participation in this evolutionary jump will turn us into experts, and cosmic specialists. Our learning process radiates out into space. We are all interlinked and interwoven in ONE. This quality of ascension will make our souls appear even more shiny and open all gates to our return into the fold of the cosmic family. What an individual does for themselves, they do for the whole. This is the great responsibility that the humans of Outer Earth are now taking over. Your heart inside you can guide you and let you walk the path of peace and respect.

My heart is filled with love. I radiate it into your hearts and your communities. May you open your hearts and enjoy this loving relationship.

Yes, the general of the heart is your future, it is the energy that will permit your future reunification with us – the people of the Agarthans and the cosmic families of Light. I must keep emphasising this. This is, after all, entirely new to the civilisations of Earth. It is a quantum leap in your connections. This energy of the heart will, of course, characterise your civilisations on Earth as well. It will bring about a respectful and supportive exchange.

We are ONE Earthly population that represents Earth in cosmos space, responsible for itself and the whole.

This, too, is part of the last piece of the puzzle. Global peace will stream into the human hearts and claims to power will not find any soil to grow on. Humans will be able to develop freely. This implies that humans will work for the weakest members of their societies and that they will support them. Hunger, misery and suffering will be reduced or even eliminated. A civilisation can only be as strong as its weakest members! Therefore, all will be done in future in order to strike an economic and social balance between the peoples. The wealth of each people will be weighed and measured for this, in order to achieve a balance.

Your endless wars and disputes will come to an end. Great material resources will be freed in order to support the populations. Every people will renew itself from the inside out. Eternal effects would be beside the point. The responsibility for renewal is with every single people, just as every person must ensure their own renewal. Every people and every person has their very own tradition and history on which they will base their renewal to sustainably enter New Earth and make their contribution. The current inflow of high cosmic energy will change every person and every people. A responsible mankind will develop from this. It will be a mankind that strives for new, pioneering and peaceful goals. It will be a mankind that will do everything to transform Earth for all her citizens into paradise.

These are your expectations of the future for which you are now building a foundation to give the next generations something on which to base their five-dimensional living motifs. This foundation is likely to be the most important part that you are now building for your new home. This is why you will need a conscious focus for the current changes and transformations, to allow you to take full responsibility for yourself and for the whole.

The cosmic energy that is arriving now is opening up your DNA and aligning it with the five-dimensional level. Your familiar two-string genetic structure will be connected to your ethereal, multi-dimensional structures now. You will grow into a quantum structure and emerge as a multi-dimensional being. You do not know yet know what that means. Soon, however, you will consciously take your path to enlightenment step by step and discover your as-yet unknown talents. You will be able to use the entire potential of your DNA, and the experience will leave you astonished and fascinated at once. Your perception in all areas will expand exponentially. Things you have barely dreamt of before will become feasible. This is the cosmic gift that is now reaching mankind and will spread its joy. The many transformations necessary for this will soon be a past experienced that belonged to Old Earth. You will remember that you have really always had those gifts. They were simply stored away inside you for a long time, without any access to them. You will, therebefore, use your new talents as a matter of course. They are very close to you, and you will find yourself familiar with them. Of course, you will still need some training and re-familiarisation.

This is the most fascinating thing about this new time: every human will deal with their own cosmic potential. Great wealth is approaching the humans of Outer Earth. Many new ideas, thoughts, plans, and many new goals and wishes are ahead. Your imagination will no longer be limited. All is ready for you in the Here-and-Now. All is waiting to be discovered by you. Open the gates of your limitations and flow into the era of New Earth with the high cosmic energy. Let the new diversity spoil you and enjoy living in the Here-and-Now and everywhere. Your physical feet will remain well-grounded on Terra as you expand into cosmic space and into Inner Earth to visit us. New impressions will enrich you and become part of our communities. The connection to All-That-Is will become real. It can be felt and touched.

The energy of the heart will become the vehicle, the vessel for experiencing this great adventure. It will be your guideline and direct you towards your life's goal or your calling. It is your motivation and your urge to make your life special in connection with Mother Earth and all people.

Your time of liberation has come. Spread your "wings" and fly! Your destination is in your hearts.

Another, last piece of the puzzle is your consciousness. It is now taking shape and breaking its borders. The high cosmic energy flowing in now will align your bodies and minds on the multi-dimensional level. This will reactivate your internal star seed after its long hibernation. You will once again become cosmic citizens as you have always been, though lost in the depths of matter for eons. Your consciousness will return to your origins, to integrity of your self. The experience you have made in the deep density of matter will accompany you and let you create untold riches. The descent into such a dense matter with the accordingly high polarity requires courage and the will to persevere. This experience will soon be a thing of the past for you. You will now be allowed to admit the higher cosmic levels of being. The divine seed that you have sown in dense matter can now develop and be brought to bloom. The cycle of Old Earth had its place. It was part of the plan of creation, just as your ascension into higher dimensional levels is now. We, the Agarthans, remained on the high vibrational level and acted as an energetic compensation for all populations, and for Mother Earth, during these dark times.

Creation is a synthesis of the arts that is well orchestrated. Everything is connected to everything else. It is a unity of divine grace where coincidence has no place. Certain processes may appear chaotic to you, yet they are entirely justified from a multi-dimensional perspective. They are part of the plan of creation.

Multi-dimensionality differs greatly from linear thinking as humans currently practice it. Soon, you will venture into this unlimited space again as well. You will remember your experiences in this respect, which are stored deeply in your DNA. Your DNA has all your memories and experiences, no matter if they come from Earth or from cosmic space. The current thrust of consciousness will return all your experiences to you. You, in turn, will be able to provide them to New Earth and her humans. This personal departure will return you to yourself – to what you have always been. To that divine being that manifests here on Earth as co-creator, for the glory of the ONE, our source. The circle of dense matter has closed. A new era is waiting to be creatively accessed.

Some innovations will now become evident in your everyday lives, your bodies and your minds. These innovations are targeted at New Earth and will now try to get a foothold here on Earth. These innovations are connected to an awakened human consciousness and a new alignment of Mother Earth with the high cosmic energy. Any sort of upheaval will help give birth to these innovations. They are, in a way, the natural consequence of the current great changes. In personal and global matters alike, a new consensus will be found to support humans and Mother Earth in a sustainable manner. You will notice that you can only live good and fulfilled lives if you take care of your environment. You will find that that concern cannot be limited within country or continental borders. We are one global Earthly population in Inner and on Outer Earth. This awareness is starting to take a hold throughout your societies now. It will lead to great economic and social consequences. All that happens in one part of Earth has global effects in every respect. Therefore, personal responsibility towards oneself, one's society and Earth will now become concrete and unavailable. Accepting personal responsibility is the prerequisite for the new era and the higher dimensional levels. This is a responsibility of the new era, the higher dimensional levels. All human civilisations of Outer Earth are now learning to take responsibility for oneself and for All-That-Is. They are starting to put this responsibility into practice. This is part of the new alignment of the new energy level, and a new interaction of the various nations.

If people are taking full responsibility for themselves from the inside out, they will grow strong and be able to engage in exchange with their neighbours as partners. The people will then strive for a balance that permits free exchange of goods, but also of ideas. Only free, satiated citizens will be able to sustainably control their homes and to contribute globally. Responsibility belonged to Old Earth as well, though many people were declared incompetent, immature or not equal. These levels will now disappear more and more, to give way to treating all persons as equals. Because of this, every individual will take over their personal responsibility. For many humans, this means a new learning process, but also an inner wish that will bring greater fulfilment to their lives. We are all divine souls that complete their learning processes on Earth. Every soul is empowered to pass and perform their learning processes fully responsible to the whole.

Criteria for the Future

The many inner and outer changes have transformed humans. They are now ready to enter the higher dimensional level of the Fifth Dimension, but also higher vibrational dimensions. These changes were necessary to cast off old ballast and to make space for new things. Your vessels, that is your bodies and their minds, as well as your communities, now have the space to take up the high cosmic vibration, and to energetically adjust to it. Pervasive global learning processes are now ahead for everyone. New or reborn humans will align themselves with the new, high energy, taking this path together with their community. This multi-dimensional awareness will now awaken in all Earthly communities. Great adjustments are the consequence. It is a global forward movement that is uninhibited by interests of power. After all, the many changes have shown you global cohesion.

Global environment, as well as economic and social strategies, will help humans design better lives for themselves in the Here-and-Now. They will give humans more safety and certainty to be able to take care of their families. Education for all humans will take priority, as will their interlinking. They will be globally in contact with their fellow humans, no matter where in the world they are. They will be able to engage in exchange with each other. These links are already developed, but they will continue to refine and reach every corner of Earth. The educational leap initiated in this will raise all of mankind onto a new level. All humans will contribute on this platform and be able to communicate their lifestyles and traditions. The levels formed still have much to learn as well. They can pass on their knowledge in turn. This interlinking of humans will make mankind move "closer together" and make them aware of their globality. Increasingly, humans will perceive themselves as global citizens of Earth. They will act accordingly, too. This awareness is about to awaken now, and will leave its determining mark on your futures. The need of some residents can be met quickly and directly this way. Human compassion will take on cosmic proportions and be unconditional.

Humans will understand that they are only as strong as those weakest in their community. This is why they will do all they can to strengthen mankind as a whole. The responsibility for one's neighbour knows no distance nor differences of any kind. We are all connected to each other in the ONE. Humans will now become aware of this.

Awareness of the connection to All-That-Is will move the humans of Outer Earth to develop new technologies with great care, while abandoning old, risky ones. Even though this will temporarily cause a deep cut in your comfort and your economies, you will welcome this step. You will do all that you can to research and use environmentally compatible technologies. Every country will work to its best efforts, responsible for its population but also under consideration of its neighbours, to develop sustainable energy resources. A great change of thinking is now taking hold of all humans, shifting away from a profit-oriented society to human coexistence on Earth. Interpersonal love, compassion for all of creation, is about to awaken. It will bring your civilisations together and dissolve existing limitations.

Loving exchange between the peoples will bring mankind safety, as well as wealth. This wealth will not be profit-oriented. It will be based on the products, ideas, and arts of a community that will then be exchanged with other people. It is a coexistence, an interweaving of various talents and ideas that will bring you this wealth. Being human will take the highest priority in all regions of Earth. This is your true motivation in life, or your fundamental human right. Humans will support each other, and take care of their weakest to make sure that all can enjoy this fundamental human right. The current transformation into a cosmic citizen will bring you all the mental and physical tools you need to master this global unification of the humans of Outer Earth.

It is a unity in variety that will bring you your wealth, along with the peace you are yearning for so much. This transfer to a higher level of existence is similar to rebirth of mankind. The old paradigms are no longer compatible with this high vibration, and some of them will now dissolve forcefully. This change of thinking affects every individual and all societies. You will now be faced with new ideas and facts. You will use this to create a new human civilisation of equality.

The high cosmic emanations now change every universal citizen. Every man and every woman are affected by this. Because of this, all societies will have to adapt to the new humanity, unbiased by suppressed traditions. They will dissolve and give way to the new humanity with all their creativity.

Events will happen in quick sequence worldwide and exponentially bring about a new human civilisation that is compatible to the five- and higher dimensional vibrational levels. You will now create this great awakening of humans to their star selves, and their return to paradise.

The standard for your future will be targeted at entirely different goals than you were, so far, used to on Old Earth. The cosmic energy of the heart that is now awakening in humans with unconditional love and compassion will embrace all of mankind in enormous waves. Every individual will be touched deeply. This energy will cause egocentricism to starve and make old claims to power collapse.

We are one Earthly population that will now come together in love and respect. We are setting joint standards for the future and will turn Earth back into a safe home we can be envied for.

You are the co-creators of this New Earth! Every individual will design their life responsibly for themselves and their people, and do all they can to align their everyday lives in coordination with the whole. Earth will adjust to the high cosmic energy and every human will flow with the new energy that will lead them into the new era of Earth. The energetic wave will determine the direction of your journey. You merely need to entrust yourself to this wave and to enjoy the cosmic ride. Hectic and chaotic conditions are likely to force you into calm and stillness periodically to enable you to truly ride this cosmic wave.

The more you experience this change of eras, the more will you understand the cosmic necessity of the changes. You will be a bearer of Light for your communities, lighting the path for mankind. Perceive your inner Light and radiate your Christ-consciousness into the world. Accept that this enables you to dissolve negative energies. Accept your power and change Earth to turn her into Paradise! Activate the code that is lodged deep inside your DNA and wants to be freed. Stand fully and entirely by your star-self, your I-AM-presence. The time has come to free yourself from your chrysalis.

Fly, my dear humans. Fly into your new reality. Fly into the new cosmic era of Earth, into the new Light cycle that is ahead of you. Design it to your wishes and enjoy the all-love that awakens and warms in you. All of us, citizens of Earth, are affected by this and enjoy its sweetness. The dark times are behind us. The times of separation and suffering are over. Our shared principle is moving forward, into Light into our future. May it come to be!

Diverging Energies

Energies that are unable to adjust to the high cosmic waves, or that have difficulty doing so, will be driven away and dissolve in the distance. All terrestrial energies now need a vibrational resonance compatible with the high cosmic wave in order to accompany Earth into its ascension phase. In a way, we are now observing natural selection of energies. This process will greatly support humans in their ascension. Instead of being energetically cast back and forth, they will be able to focus on their own personal paths. One could say that any energies deviating from the cosmic vibrational amplitude will be unable to connect to the higher level of existence. They cannot cross the gate into the new era as a result. Because of this, the range of energies will only be suitable for a five-dimensional level starting at a certain frequency. The vibrational heaviness of the third and fourth dimensions is dissolving and disappearing. Humans on that vibrational heaviness will require great transformation work to climb up their path to the new octave, provided that they want to do this. Generally, the higher vibrational level is open to every human. The transformations they need for this may differ greatly, however.

Your transfer into the new era will be easier the more Light particles you integrate in your bodies and minds. This process makes you energetically selective. This means that you will attract places, people, and work of higher vibrations. You will start to find slow-vibrational experiments insufferable. This will reposition you in your community - After all, birds of a feather do flock together. You may find that long-established relationships are breaking apart. You may move away from your usual environment or change your job. Many of these things are a consequence of the high vibration you are now integrating, which is changing you even on a cellular level. First, you will still attempt to live in parallel on different energy levels. The more strongly acceleration progresses, the more difficult it will be to continue with this split within you. Your intention to walk the path of Light will help you take it without any compromises, and let go of your past. Every human is now facing this personal selection. Every human must independently come to a decision. Every human is now, after all, fully responsible.

Some people will leave the planet in future. Their souls may want to accompany the ascension from a different dimension, or the energy level of Earth may no longer be compatible with those souls. They will continue their learning processes on other three-dimensional planets.

The energies that cannot adjust to the high five-dimensional vibrations will be dissolved or transformed by them. Earth will be able to continue on her journey into Light freed of these, but with a harmonised polarity of her energies. Earth and her humans will no longer be exposed to excesses. They will continue on their journey in a harmonised polarity vibration. This means that humans are now free of all sorts of excess, such as wars, crimes, or other matters. Mankind will throw off these heavy burdens. Humans will be able to re-align themselves in a new vibrational spectrum, and turn to different types of learning processes. Balancing of the gaping polarity will let greater calm and serenity take hold of people and give them the leisure to show more of an interest in their own matters and to develop on a spiritual level. The high cosmic vibration that Earth will now reach will bring spiritual matters into your everyday lives and your communities. The higher cosmic perspective of our creator will become part of your thoughts and activities. It will contribute to giving humans the feeling of being connected to, and supported by, All-That-Is. The consequences of this philosophy, which will be new to many, will design the structure of New Earth under entirely different aspects than you have been used so far. The separation from Old Earth is complete. New holistic conditions are taking over the construction of your new societies in economic, social and religious respects. You will be growing out of frozen structures and liberated from restrictive and manipulative traditions.

The new humans will no longer allow any sort of suppression. They have fully stepped into their cosmic responsibility towards themselves and their communities. Human civilisations and societies will renew themselves from the very basics in order to permit a new collaboration on Earth. This is a process that will continue through the next years and decades. It depends on integration of the high cosmic vibration. Every person and every nation will absorb this vibration independently and transform it accordingly. As I have said: the times of potentates of power in all matters are definitely over. Every human being will feel their connection to their star-self, their soul, and know precisely what is right for them. Many will recognise their learning process and their calling that they want to experience on Earth. Adult, responsible humans will meet lovingly and lay the foundations for the "Golden Age" that will brighten up Earth and her residents for future generations. Earth as a whole is now opening the gate into the prophesied cycle of Light. Humans are accompanying her with good will.

The new, high cosmic vibrations reach all cells and atoms of humans and of Earth. They will transform and spiritualise the planet and her residents, in order to align them with the reality of energy. The current changes on Earth, and those of the last years, must be viewed under this consensus. They are not due to karma. Mother Earth is worried about her residents. She does not want to harm them. Greater upheaval is therefore always preceded by warnings, such as increased seismic activity and volcanic eruptions. Your animals and plants have sensors that you have forgotten how to use. Watch your birds and undomesticated animals attentively. Changes in their behaviour will warn you. The humans must learn to live increasingly with nature, and to sharpen their senses. All living creatures have special sensors. They are all closely connected to Mother Earth. Bring your feelings and your reason into your hearts. Act based on them. A good connection to Earth will bring stability for every human in a time that is changing so quickly. Listen to the indigenous peoples of Earth. They have continued to develop with Mother Earth. Now, they will be able to support the rational societies and point the way back to her.

This time of transition conceals pervasive personal and global learning processes. Humans will re-learn living with Earth and her rhythms, adjusting their activities to the planet. The terrestrial cycles are long and have their own paradigms that are worth being explored, even by a population that is present there only for a relatively brief period of time. They are responsible for the well-being of their further generations. Earth will retain her place in the cosmos. Humans may destroy their right to live on Terra, however. This awareness will awaken in all humans now, preventing exploitation of resources or atomic energy generation rendering life on Terra impossible for future generations. The responsibility of every individual goes beyond their lifetime on Earth, but also includes future generations. Mankind must learn to think and act in larger cycles, and to question short-term scenarios that are negative for Earth. Everyone is needed for this process. They may need to step out of their comfort zone. New and holistic energy resources will return prosperity. An intermediate bottleneck should not deter you in light of the well-being of future generations. Leaving old habits is also part of the process you are going through with Earth now. You will be renewed and move on with New Earth, creating the tools you need in light of All-That-Is.

The range of energies will change drastically now, allowing you to enter higher vibrational levels. This will cause power scenarios to dissolve, along with criminal actions. These energies of higher vibrations will also help you balance out your bodies and minds. This will initiate a comprehensive process of healing. As the name says, healthcare will deal with healthy persons. Prevention of diseases will become more and more important, every person will be responsible. They will contribute to going along their paths in life in a healthy manner. Genetic diseases will be researched and healed as well. Humans will be researched in their holistic context, rather than merely to counter symptoms. The increased vibration will achieve many scientific breakthroughs in all matters in future, to benefit mankind and all its civilisations. Harmonisation of polarities will provide new scenarios for better energetic support. Many old dependencies dissolve to liberate the new human. Humans are once again come into their original power. They will help design new Earth, responsible for the whole. Cosmic laws will express their divine co-creatorship. The re-design of human societies will be driven accordingly. Life models will change, supported by rewritten laws. Your communities will be re-organised and re-structured - they must adjust to the new human after all.

Great global projects will bring humans more closely together. The mutual energy of the heart will connect humans and promote the humanitarian, cultural and economic exchange. No matter where they are at home, humans will feel safe in the global community of Earth. They will feel the strength of mutual commitment and take strength from it for their own lives. The cooperation of the population of Earth will characterise the development of New Earth.

The exchange of scientific and technological findings will become a matter of course. The future of Earth and her humans, rather than your personal or national interests, will take priority in future. These are far-reaching deviations from your current structures, yet the high cosmic vibration that you are now all integrating will make the impossible possible with the great leap of consciousness that you are now experiencing.

Earth and her humans are now exposed to considerable energetic acceleration that will continued through another few years and decades. This time will, by necessity, bring about pervasive changes and position you on a new vibrational level. This is a cosmic leap of evolution that takes hold of Earth and her humans. It is the alignment with Light that was prophesied by your old scriptures and that is now coming true. Enjoy this intense time and let its energy carry and nurture you. Harvest the fruits that you sowed eons ago. You created the unimaginable. You are cosmic masters of Light. We thank you out of our whole hearts for your unceasing, loving commitment. Light and love have won the battle against darkness!

Acceptance of the Inevitable

As I have said before, the time of great changes has a cosmic origin. The entire solar system, and even its direct galactic zone, are now moving closer to the Light of their central sun, and also their galactic centre. This must greatly influence the vibrational quality of the affected celestial bodies. The vibrational amplitude is raised by this. The current increase of the Earthly vibration will lift Terra onto a new, multi-dimensional octave of being. The old, restrictive quality of being will be cut away and dissolved. Earth is now undergoing a great evolutionary leap. Earth is now aligning herself with this high vibration. Changes to Earth, shifts of the axis of Earth, and anomalous weather are inevitable.

My dear people of Outer Earth: try to look at the past and future changes from this point of view. Every single person knows on the level of their soul what they have signed up for in their incarnation. Every person had the free will to contribute to this transition to a higher octave of being, on one or the other side of the veil. Be certain that the many people who die in dramatic events will return home and support Earth and her people from that dimension. They have been liberated and they are well. Let this be consolation in your grief. Humans are immortal. Death merely liberates them from their bodies, their Earthen vessels. Their personalities and love remain with them on their further journeys into Light. With their deaths on Earth, humans produce a great wave of compassion and solidarity in times of disaster. Human societies and nations move closer together and support each other in this way. The hearts of humans around the world are also touched and opened. This, too, is part of the intended change towards a higher dimension. The humans on Outer Earth will continue to take their path on the level of the heart. Such events also prepare humans, among other things, to this new aspect. The multi-dimensional level of existence will show you that we are all connected to each other in love and to our divine source and origin. This connection and love now opens to the humans of Outer Earth. It will unite nations, which will live in great responsibility and respect, in harmony with our Mother Earth.

Refusal of integrating this current high vibration and facing the pending personal and global changes will put great pressure on humans and their societies. Their behaviour will not be compatible with New Earth. Eventually, all societies and their humans will have to align themselves with the new energy if they want to survive this transition or rebirth in the higher form of existence. There will be some lagging behind here and there. The Earthly community will have to carry them along. It will be a challenge for all of you. However, do not forget that every human and every nation must develop from the inside. Interventions will no longer be tolerated. Also remember, however, that young people from those nations already bear the five-dimensional seeds inside themselves. They will ensure that old claims to power in their societies will be broken up and new structures developed. The young generations around the world are prepared very well for this change. They will become the persons responsible in your future communities. They will make the five-dimensional seeds bloom and contribute their multi-dimensional heritage. Trust in this young generation and support them with your vision. Of course, pioneers of dimensional changes live among the older generations as well. They have worked towards this evolutionary leap all their lives. They had to tolerate plenty of rejection, derision, and intolerance. Now, they will finally be able to harvest the fruits of their hard work, and support the young generations in development.

On the level of souls, many old souls are currently active in this dimensional change. The Earthly age of a human is therefore rendered relative in this time of development. The soul families now come together to actively support and implement this building and rebirth. The soul families can be made up of entirely different incarnation options, on Earth as well as in cosmic space or in Inner Earth. The souls that belong to one family will now be consciously reunited. Do not be surprised if you feel particularly drawn to a specific planet or to Inner Earth. The affiliation of your soul is starting to manifest now. The veil of forgetting will dissolve step by step and will consciously reunite you with your family of souls. All of us, all residents of our universe, are ONE in the ONE. Our star siblings accompany our evolutionary leap here on Earth. Their love supports our efforts and strengthens us in our task of higher-dimensional re-orientation.

Your readiness to adjust to the high cosmic energy will align your minds and your bodies with the new vibrational amplitude. This is a process in which you will be confronted with old mental patterns that are now dissolved and transformed. These transformations will feel like a remedy for your bodies. They will be cleaned of many old wastes, to become better prepared for integrating the high energy. This energetic integration of high cosmic vibration will align your bodies multi-dimensionally. This means that your DNA will now be able to unfold for the new vibrational levels. The result of this process of unfolding is difficult to put into words for three- and four-dimensionally vibrating humans. However, I would like to offer you a metaphor to explain your new status of existence. Imagine a room in which have been locked for eons. You have furnished it comfortably, but you were completely separated from the outer world. Now, windows and doors of that room open, and you can see that you are living in a house. You have neighbours. The sun is shining, and you can enjoy an unrestricted view, spot colours, and hear sounds that were entirely unknown to you before. An overwhelming variety is ready for you to explore and discover. Of course it will take courage and trust to leave this familiar room and entirely venture into such new situations of life. However, please remember that you were originally once multi-dimensionally aligned. Exploration of the dense matter led you into your state of amnesia. This time has now finally come to an end. You will now once again be able to connect to your multi-dimensional heritage. You will remember that cosmic condition. The time of liberation will make you euphoric. You will feel that you are on the way back to yourself. You are coming back home. The learning goals, lessons, and talents that you have mastered in the past will once again be available to you. This precious treasure is now given to the human civilisations. They will develop into a multi-dimensional Earthly community, connected with, and linked to, All-That-Is. The cosmic unconditional love will fill your hearts again, and compassion will guide your actions and activities. A multi-dimensional being is filled with love.

They will become a conscious co-creator of their reality, and feel commitment to the greater whole.

Dare to venture out of your room, my dear humans of Outer Earth! A wonderful future is waiting for you to explore.

Your bodies are very special tools that enable your incarnation. Integration of the high cosmic energy will leave you amazed at what your bodies can do with their intelligence. They will be able to heal themselves from diseases and delay their aging process. They will also be able to feel their environment and any dangers. They will also be able to let the cosmic Light and energies of Mother Earth shine through them. Your bodies are your connection between Mother Earth and heaven. Just look at the divine creations you have been given for your path on Earth! Honour it and treat it with respect. Feed it, move it, exercise it, and take care of it. Every individual body has its own needs that need to be discovered. Let it have the rest and stillness that it yearns for to powerfully serve you once again. Your bodies need your love and attention more than anything else. They are your divine temples. They are your way of manifesting here on Earth. Your divine spirits and your bodies merge for one phase of incarnation. This symbiosis allows you to master your desired learning goal and to connect to your follow humans on the level of existence on Earth. They allow you to love and be loved. Remember the many wonderful touches that you have been allowed to receive in your lives. Remember the sunlight, rain and water, or the wind that you have been able to feel on your bodies. Remember warmth and cold, dryness and moisture. All of these are experiences that your body has given you. They are exhilarating moments that make your soul rejoice. Yes, it is your greatest asset here on Earth. It is the perfect way to manifest your souls. These divine gifts are like creation itself, an expression of our living source. Every human is divine and deserves the respect and honour to match. We are all divine attributes on our missions on Earth. We have all been created in love and our bodies are perfect ways to spread this divine love on Earth, by smiles, touches or embraces.

Your bodies are the vessels of your souls, or your spirits. Let them shine through your bodies and touch your fellow humans with your divine presence. These divine sparks will merge to create New Earth, the future Golden Age: Paradise.

Five-Dimensional Vibration Levels

For quite some time, the cosmic emanations of our sun have accelerated the Earth's vibrations. Now, this acceleration has markedly increased. The time of dimensional change is just ahead. The winter solstice of 2012 represents the beginning of the new high level of existence. This does not mean that the Earthly vibration will moderate itself again afterwards. Quite the opposite: Vibration will continue to accelerate, stabilising at a high level around 2025. After that, vibration will continue to accelerate at a more moderate pace. After all, evolution is always connected to a progression of the vibrational amplitude.

The next years and decades will, therefore, continue to be characterised by changes and challenges for humans. First, you need to let go of old structures and create new ones – both on personal and global levels. Earth and humans must integrate this high vibration. This is an adjustment process that challenges Earth and her humans, but is also aligned with the new energy. This is a pervasive process that spiritualises all of matter. Humans are, in a way, mutating into a higher octave of being with their living bodies. Earth plays her part in adjusting to the cosmic community.

The transition phase until the end of 2012 will likely be the most difficult period. Once the Fifth Dimension commences, mostly energetic adjustments and implementation of new structures will occur on a daily basis. Humans must learn to handle the new, spiritualising matter and the social, political, economic, and religious changes. Humans across the globe will be challenged by enormous reconstruction work following earthquakes. The countries will be unable to manage their destructions on their own. They will receive global compassion and help. This will throw humans out of their territorial concerns and connections, leading them into global perspectives. Earth as a whole will keep humans busy. The different civilisations and traditions will clasp hands and a wave of compassion will open the hearts of humans. Future cooperation will take place on the level of the heart, which is the foundation of a five-dimensional plane of existence.

The many structural changes, as well as the lives on a changing Earth, will teach humans to live in the Here-and-Now and to prepare for new things from this perspective. Flexibility and alertness will be necessary to easily traverse this time.

The five-dimensional level will, for the first time, enable you to return to multi-dimensional regions. It is, in a way, the jumping board into the higher dimensions. This is why the current evolutionary leap is of unimaginable importance for Earth. You are now truly leaving a limited plane in order to engage in free future development. This implies a firm anchor on Mother Earth. She will give you the stability to move into unrestricted realms. With your feet firmly rooted on Terra, you will be able to venture into the heavens with all of their dimensions. You will be able to enrich Earth with this. On your path into unlimited realms, be they micro- or macrocosmic, you will see that this will only be possible with an awakened spirituality. Creation is the loving expression of the ONE, the source of all of us.

Research and science will witness this all-encompassing love. Their work will bear witness to this. This high cosmic perspective will flow into your philosophies and influence everyday human lives. This higher view of belonging together in love and compassion will strengthen your societies and serve as a guideline for your cohabitation. The point of view will reform your religions and raise them up to a five-dimensional level. The global religions will pay special attention to the love for All-That-Is and connect through it. Each religion will preserve its own rituals, but exercise them in a holistic context. The different religions are linked to the local tradition. They will, however, shift to a cosmic alignment. Divine love and compassion for all of creation will enter Earth comprehensively. They will change civilisations in their image. Cosmic Christ will once again be at home in your hearts.

The community on Earth will renew itself from the heart. It will adjust its societal, social, religious and economic structures accordingly. The known excesses of the third dimension will be unable to pass through the five-dimensional gate. They will not be energetically compatible and will be unable to withstand a harmonised polarity.

Dear humans, look forward to his new era of Earth. Pain and suffering will cease to be part of your everyday lives. Peace and joy will replace them. The energy acquired from harmonisation of polarities will flow into your peace-loving and sustainable projects. Life on Earth will become simpler and more harmonious for every individual.

The five-dimensional octave of being is bringing about spiritualisation of matter, leading to many innovations in its handling. The more spiritualised matter is, the easier it will be to handle. Agricultural cultivation, technical products, architectural and artistic projects and much more will become much easier to implement for you.

Spiritualised matter will react to your state of mind and can be influenced by the power of thoughts, you will, in a way, spiritually connect to matter and create your sustainable projects with this support. The timelessness of the Here-and-Now will receive the impulse, and the energy will flow into this feasibility strategy. The higher vibration of matter will facilitate execution. Matter can be better modelled and easier handled. The quality of separation of Old Earth is dissolved and a new connection to Earth and its matter is necessary. The higher the vibration of matter and beings, the better they are connected to each other; the better they can adjust to each other and implement spiritual impulses. The matter of Earth will be a partnership of humans in development and the cleansing of New Earth. It will teach humans about this new way of handling it. The population of Earth is in urgent need of clean habitats to feed itself and to survive.

This new research will involve all of your wise people, no matter if they hail from science or from alternative sides, such as the indigenous people or the sensitives. An integrated approach to cleansing Mother Earth should be considered. The various types of pollution (atomic and chemical toxins, etc.) of Old Earth have severely damaged the planet. The five-dimensional plane will no longer accept any technologies that would harm humans and Earth. It will, however, also support humans in their motivation and implementation of cleansing Earth. New five-dimensional technologies will become established and help you with this!

Mother Earth will introduce you to this cleaning process. Your symbiosis with her will now become truly practiced, both materially and emotionally. The new way of handling our planet will no longer be determined by reason alone, but also by a deep emotional and spiritual connection to Earth. This is the prerequisite for a growing five-dimensional level. Everything is connected to everything in the love of our creator.

The beginning of the five-dimensional vibrational level will greatly challenge you. The wastes of Old Earth must be transformed and removed in order to leave behind an Earth worth living on for your next generations.

The living situations will now be continually raised in terms of vibration. This means that your interpersonal contacts will also develop into a new level of coexistence. Aggression, power, envy, and jealousy will disappear from your relationships. They are no longer compatible with the new vibrational level. Interest, compassion, and cordiality will replace them. Your social connections will be recognised and experienced as the network that gives your comfort, stability, and strength.

The energy of the heart will characterise all of your personal, social, and national relationships, and accordingly also have a global effect. A multicultural Earth community united in their hearts will take care of the well-being of Mother Earth, and give all populations a feeling of strength and stability. An Earth civilisation united on the level of the heart will support those who are the weakest and share their riches. This conscious mankind will also be ready to venture into the cosmic space and to contact their star families and the population of the Agarthans. Your star families are already represented on Earth, just as we already telepathically connect to you. Perceive the many messages that are now sent through channellings. Feel your way into them and get to know your cosmic brothers and sisters, as well as us, the Agarthans.

This option enables you to prepare for your cosmic contact, and to already receive new technologies for the reconstruction of your societies and for cleansing of the Earth. The cosmic family has multi-dimensional technologies that they will gladly share with the Earthly family, in order to enable it to successfully cleanse itself of the wastes of Old Earth. We are all connected in the ONE and support each other in this scope. Just as you support your weakest members, we support you on your journey into Light. Of course, this is always subject to the proviso of free will. Never will any cosmic or innerterrestrial nation intervene in your lives. You are the captains of Outer Earth. You will say what help you want to accept. Know that we are all willing to support you in love, without any colonialist desires. We do not know such ambitions. They belong in a lower vibrational level.

The new era on Earth breaks through old structures and behaviours. Therefore, entirely new, loving procedures still feel suspicious to you. The increase of your vibrational level will resolve this dilemma as well, developing you into loving cosmic citizens, for which the energy of the heart becomes established as a basis of their interactions.

The many terrestrial changes through earthquakes and climate-related destruction, as well as due to human technical failure, will cause a great wave of compassion throughout the global population. You will be forced to face the fact that you are all connected, no matter the long distances that separate you. This compassion will open the hearts of humans. They will do all they can to support a population that has been afflicted.

Any event also has a positive side to it. These disasters will bring humans closer to each other again, in love. That love and the responsibility towards all of mankind will motivate you to rethink your energetic resources and to produce new energy with the same high yield but greater sustainability. This change to sustainable energy resources is now being strongly enforced all around. Thanks to the high accelerated vibration, it can be implemented quickly. The expected energetic shortfall will be brief. However, it will force you to rethink your consumption habits and to initiate adjustments. This surely will not be easy for a spoiled, carefree society. However, this shows just how unconsciously you have gone about your lives without considering possible consequences. A responsible human society must think about their actions in a holistic manner and come to respectful conclusions. This is the process that you are now facing in this time of transfer. It is a task you need to solve. This is surely a great challenge for every person, and in particular for urban, industrialised societies that have lost sight of their relationship with Mother Earth and that have become committed to a profit-oriented scenario. This will change economic priorities, they need to give way to different priorities. Holistic approaches and structures are being developed in order to allow future generations to live on Earth as well. Such considerations are still new for you. However, the variety of man-made pollutants will be your incentive. The future suffering of your children and grandchildren will not leave you untouched. This will lead to a comprehensive change of political thinking. Innovative, holistic energy resources will be subsidised, researched, and implemented. A long learning process will be fulfilled.

Humans have taken responsibility for themselves and their home planet. This is the basis of a five-dimensional vibrational level.

As mentioned, mankind will develop from the inside out. A pervasive process of maturation is currently taking place in every individual, initiated and supported by the high, accelerated cosmic vibration.

The Interplay of Worlds

The cosmos and our universe are inhabited by billions of planets and their populations. They are a gigantic conglomeration of energies, ranging from the lowest to the highest dimensions, with their different energy densities and corresponding learning processes.

Our dear home planet, named Earth, Terra, or Gaia, gives her various populations the corresponding learning processes based on their dimensional qualities and the matching energy density. The populations of Outer Earth have acquired a three- and four-dimensional learning experience, with vastly separated polarities, over the eons following their fall into the deeper matter. This learning experience now comes to an end. Five-dimensional impressions will replace it. This scenario has a cosmic background that I have already explained. We of Inner Earth have continued to develop for eons in the five-dimensional vibrational density. We are approaching the end of this learning experience. We have held the five-dimensional quality for you during this time and are now able to support you in this dimensional transition.

We were always closely connected to you during our long separation. We know the journey of your fate well.

We, the residents of Earth, are all siblings. We are very happy that you are going on this journey back to your original status of being. We will help you to the best of our ability, but without trying to manipulate you or to intervene physically. We are giving you energetic starting support and will accompany you with our love. We are very proud of your efforts, of your success in holding the divine Light and love even in the darkest times, and that you are now able to follow Earth into the higher octave of being.

A long period of linear understanding of time is now nearing its end. We are not affected by this quality of time. We are waiting for your return as if you were coming back home after an extended journey. Our arms are open wide in joyful expectation of a mutual embrace. We will have a lot to tell each other. Our mutual experiences will enrich each other. Together, we will take our planet's fate into our hands. We will prepare a happy and fulfilled future for our children to let them develop further with a home that is worth living in.

The different worlds of our cosmos are populated with many different residents. They are all part of the divine spark that created us all. We all make many different learning experiences in order to enrich our Father/Mother God and to finally reunite him/her. Our divine exploration brings us into contact with many different dimensional densities and their energy qualities. Every divine spark is trying to manifest the creative power on its own matter. We are all divine co-creators in this cosmic game, yet we all remain eternally connected to this source. We all enter into the illusion of matter, model it, and then return to our origin, to the All-Love. Accordingly, we carry love into matter; into creation. The divine spark of love is present in all of us, even in the very dense dimensions. The higher a dimension is vibrating, the more aware we will be of this divine mission of love and the responsibility connected to it.

The pending dimensional change of Earth will rouse the residents of Outer Earth from their hibernation and make them aware of their mission of love. This energy of love will ignite the hearts of people again and animate them to align their societies with these vibrations of love. This is the reason for the comprehensive, political, economic and social turbulences that you are meeting now. This is an adjustment to the divine vibration of love that reaches you now through the cosmic emanations. You are witnesses of a great divine romance that you can actively help design. Your creativity will no longer know any bounds, it is integral to the cosmic plan and free to unfold.

All of us – residents of the cosmic worlds – are divine lovers in action. We are the expression of our source, or origin. We are all eternally connected to each other in this love. We create our Garden Eden, our paradise, no matter where we are at home. Where love rules, we are connected to our divine origin, and able to practice it in our lives.

The residents of Outer Earth will now take the quantum leap of the loving hearts. Like a domino effect, the hearts of humans will once again open to the divine All-Love and abandon themselves to the flow of love that will anchor their new lives. Love has once again caught up with the population of Earth. Love will ensure well-being of our home planet and love will reunite us as siblings. Love is the basis for all future interactions and our existence. Feel it, breathe it, and spread it. The more you give, the more it will give to you in turn! It is a cosmic cycle!

Cosmic love will break through your old societal paradigms and give way to a new human cohabitation. This need will spread from every individual, developing from their inner-most core. True, pervasive changes are only credible and sustainable in this manner. The new societal structures will slowly adjust to the high cosmic vibration and the humans involved. A pervasive learning process will take hold of the terrestrial civilisations. High media linkage will allow it to quickly bear fruit. In contrast to generations of the past, the current changes will not take several generations for implementation. Humans are now ready for this implementation. They even yearn to finally be able to live with a compatible societal, economic and social structure. The actual revolution or rebirth will take place inside every individual. All that remains to be done then is adjustment of their respective structures in life.

A population that vibrates on five-dimensional levels will quickly continue on its evolution. For the first time, it will have multi-dimensional magnitudes at its disposal that it can research and study. Terrestrial borders will be easier to overcome. Contact with the cosmic star family is a natural consequence and future. The old veil of separation will fall from your eyes and clear your view into multi-dimensional levels.

A great awakening will happen for the humans of Outer Earth. They will acquire certainty of interplay of the cosmic worlds and their populations, no matter if they are living on or in a planet, just as we live in Inner Earth. The new multi-dimensional understanding will involve our existence as well and promote our future contacts. At this time, we can only present this path to you; however, look at the mythologies of the indigenous peoples with whom we have always stayed connected.

The time of our mutual contact is finally coming closer. We are greatly looking forward to direct contact with our terrestrial siblings again, to engage in exchange, and to unite in divine love. The populations of Inner and Outer Earth will heal our Mother Earth of the wastes of Old Earth and let her mature again into the Garden Eden for all of us. Our future generations should, and may once again, enjoy her as the basis of the development of their souls and experience the prophesied "Golden Age of Earth" with her.

Some of us will come again to enjoy the fruits of our long incarnations on Earth. Others will go home to their original star siblings to tell about the victory of Light on Earth and to share the experiences they have gained there. All of them will find this dimensional change a mystery, an initiation into multi-dimensional levels, a relationship of love with All-That-Is.

My dear people, may the love of the people of the Agarthans warm and open your hearts. May our energy support you in this time of great change, and may our shared love radiate into cosmic space, supporting our dear Mother Earth on her journey.

Together, we are a jewel of divine creation. Let us let the cosmic worlds participate in this and embrace them in love.

Alao*,

(*Meaning: wholeheartedly, with all my heart)

Your brother, Rodon of Agartha.

Acknowledgement

My dear niece Melody Aimée Reymond made it possible for me to publish this book in this manner. I thank her wholeheartedly for her commitment, her motivation and her unceasing effort.

Other Books by the Same Author

Intergalactic Cooperation
Messages of Ashtar Sheran

I, Ashtar Sheran, have been closely connected to the cosmos in love since its very beginning. It is my task to give Light its place, and to guide and support Earth and her people into this ascension into the Fifth Dimension. Mankind is now ready for this evolutionary leap and to take responsibility for their future. We are all connected in the ONE and welcome the residents of Earth in the galactic family.

In this book, I would like to provide some information that will help you leave behind your island existence and contact your star siblings. Break through your limitations and accept your multi-dimensional heritage! We are all connected to, and interwoven with, each other. We are creating the new Heaven and the new Earth together. Your divine nature will enter even your smallest atom and imbue you with new strength.

Love is the quintessence of all of creation. Without love, the cosmos would dissolve!

Harmonisation of the Polarities

Messages from Sekhmet

I have been connected to mankind in love for eons. I gladly take the dimensional change as an inspiration to explain the situation or the upcoming changes to you, my dear people, in order to let you accept and integrate this ascension into the Fifth Dimension and handle this new energy with elegance and dignity. The love of your star siblings is very present here on Earth. They support you where they can and are permitted to. After all, they, too, continually progress on their own evolutionary spirals.

You are developing together with your cosmic family. Only together with the other carriers of Light will you be able to ascend on the evolutionary spiral. Our hearts meet in the ONE, to permit Light-filled ascension of our entire universe.

Be aware of your responsibility for the whole and continue with Earth on your cosmic journey into Light. Our mutual love nurtures and invigorates us for the glory of the ONE. A wonderful new Earthly cycle is about to commence. It will guide humans into the Golden Era. Praised be the carriers of Light that permit this evolutionary leap for humans.

In deepest gratitude and love,
Sekhmet.

Help for Ascension into the 5th Dimension

Messages from Sirius A

Earth and her humans are about to complete a dimensional change. This is why the time in which we are now living on Earth is rich in transformation. The Sirians want to help us humans during this important time of transition. We are equal space siblings. With their brief statements, they aim to specifically reach people who do not have the time to deal more intensely with the subject of dimensional change. These are instructions for a time of pervasive changes.

We all contribute in the Light of the ONE. We are all connected to each other. Love will keep us together forever.

Printed in Great Britain
by Amazon